WARNINGS FROM THE GARDEN

UNCOVERING THE WILES OF DECEPTION

Tavares D. Robinson

Published by Watchman Publishing
www.watchmanpublishing.com
1-800-714-3194

Watchman Publishing is a Christian publisher that seeks to edify the local church by equipping individuals. We provide resources to admonish, exhort, reprove, and encourage the church in the Last Days.

WARNINGS FROM THE GARDEN: UNCOVERING THE WILES OF DECEPTION

Copyright © 2019 by Tavares D. Robinson

ISBN: 978-1-7325134-2-6

Unless otherwise noted, Scripture is taken from the Holy Bible, New King James Version®. Copyright © 1982 by Thomas Nelson. Used by permission. All rights reserved.

Scripture noted as NIV is from the Holy Bible, New International Version®, NIV® Copyright ©1973, 1978, 1984, 2011 by Biblica, Inc.® Used by permission. All rights reserved worldwide.

Scripture noted as NLT is from the Holy Bible, New Living Translation, copyright © 1996, 2004, 2015 by Tyndale House Foundation. Used by permission of Tyndale House Publishers, Inc., Carol Stream, Illinois 60188. All rights reserved.

All rights reserved. No part of this book may be reproduced or transmitted in any form or by any means, electronic, mechanical, photocopying, and recording, or by any information storage or retrieval system, except as may be expressly permitted in writing by the publisher or by U.S.A. copyright law.

Cover and interior design: Terry Bailey

Editors: Carolyn Stanford Goss and Leonard G. Goss, GoodEditors.com, www.goodeditors.com

First Printing 2019 / Printed in the United States of America

Acknowledgments

I would like to thank my friend and editor, Leonard Goss. May the Lord reward you for your enduring labor. Aslan is on the move.

To Jayda Hall, thank you for your work in producing the manuscript. Without your sacrifice this book would not have been possible. The providence of God is greater than we can see or understand. May the Lord use your gifting for his service.

Most important, to my Lord and Savior Jesus Christ. Thank you for trusting me with another message. To serve you is not just a privilege; it's an honor. May the Lamb of God receive the reward of his suffering.

TABLE OF CONTENTS

Introduction 7

The Prep Course 17
The Pathology of a Lie 31
The Ploy 41
Propaganda 47
Perversion of Adam and Eve 51
Perception and Perspective 59
The Particulars of Deception 65
The Pinball of Punishment 71
The Posterior of Adam 79
The Provenance of Disobedience 85
Preventative Measures 93
Prevail in Warfare 97

About the Author 103
Other Titles by Tavares Robinson 104

Teaching establishes you,
while warnings help protect what was built in you.

INTRODUCTION

The church and culture have entered into a dark and immoral era that I call the post-age epoch—a gradual shift from postmodern, to post-Christian, and now post-truth worldviews. But exactly what do these three terms mean?

Postmodernism posits that absolute truth is unattainable. All truth, all morality, is relative. Truth is subject to one's own experience. What is right or wrong is whatever works for us individually. Postmodernism posits that there are no moral absolutes. (Ironically, saying there are no absolutes is an absolute statement.) For postmoderns—who reject absolutes and favor subjectivity—everything is arbitrary. They believe meaning and morality are merely constructs of a society.

In a *post-Christian* era, reality is understood through physical observations and natural phenomena (science), and an individual's beliefs, feelings, and rights are paramount. While a post-Christian society is rooted in Christianity, this worldview rejects biblical authority in favor of current or popular trends. In fact, its view of Christianity is one of ridicule and contempt. Christians themselves no longer consider the language and beliefs of post-Christianity Christian.

In 2016, Oxford University Press selected the term *post-truth* as its "international word of the year." Living in a post-truth age is living in a world where truth and facts are obsolete. This mode of thought holds that objective facts are less important than one's opinions, beliefs, or feelings. Perception triumphs over reality in the post-truth age. It's an age in which dishonesty is considered harmless, especially if it helps to fulfill one's own objectives. Simply put, the post-truth age is an age of glorified deception.

When Deception Was Evil

Deception was not always the commonly accepted way to live, run a business, serve as a public official, or function as a Christian. There was a time when deception was considered unethical and downright evil—but no longer. Now many who ought to be following Christ's example openly embrace and justify anti-Christian character and behavior. This is what happens whenever the church starts following the leadership of the culture and sacrificing historical biblical truths on the altar of relativism and trendiness.

Because of postmodern, post-Christian, and post-truth ideologies, the modern church—the "set apart" ones—has traded its unique commission—to be salt and light in the world, to expose darkness, and to collect its birthright of a heavenly home—for open-mindedness, inclusiveness, non-judgmentalism, conformity, and a longing desire for the here and now. In essence, we have become the twenty-first century version of Esau.

The family line of Esau is found in the book of Genesis, chapter thirty-six. Scripture identifies Esau as a man who valued his current times over an eternal reward. He valued the seen over the unseen, and he forfeited what was permanent to gratify his temporary desires and ambitions (Hebrews 12:15–17). This is what the post-truth mindset has brought into the church.

Ignorance of biblical history—or in some cases, historical amnesia—has left the church vulnerable to the ever-changing current of the culture. There are few things the Enemy enjoys more than

God's people being historically illiterate. English novelist and cultural critic George Orwell wrote: "To enforce the lies of the present, it is necessary to erase the truths from the past. Who controls the past controls the future. Who controls the present controls the past." G. K. Chesterton, an English writer, poet, and theologian, expressed the same point: "The disadvantage of men not knowing the past is that they do not know the present. History is a hill or high point of vantage, from which alone men see the town in which they live or the age in which they are living. Without some such contrast or comparison, without some shifting of the point of view, we should see nothing." Likewise, C. S. Lewis, a British writer, theologian, and apologist, wrote frequently about what he called "the great cataract of nonsense," our tendency to concern ourselves only with the present and divorce ourselves from the past. Lewis' prophetic statement still rings true in our era, for to truly understand our current times we need a historical perspective. Divorcing ourselves from the past makes us blind in the present. Furthermore, believers without knowledge of the past are spiritual infants in the hands of the Ancient Seducer and Fallen Angel. In the Scriptures we see that every time God's people forgot their history, apathy, anarchy, apostasy, and abandonment soon followed. And whenever the church turns her back on history, she will embrace appealing spokespersons who teach a future devoid of any type of reality.

The Post-Truth Movement Is Not New

Undermining the authority of Scripture in order to exalt human autonomy is not a new thing. King Solomon said, "History merely repeats itself. It has all been done before. Nothing under the sun is truly new. Sometimes people say, 'Here is something new!' But actually it is old; nothing is ever truly new" (Ecclesiastes 1:9–10 NLT). The waves of post-truth have steadily made their way into the church, disarming our discernment and desensitizing us to damnable teachings.

The post-truth movement is actually rooted in the Garden of Eden, where the idea of sin was foreign. The concept of post-truth was crafted by a supernatural being who relied on an exceptionally cunning serpent to carry it out. The Garden was the original dwelling place for the first human pair, Adam and Eve, who were created sinless by God and who dwelled in an environment God called good. Adam and Eve became the first victims of a post-truth mindset when the Serpent moved them away from a theocentric view of the world to a humanistic one. God, and the authority of his Word, was no longer the centerpiece of their lives; self had become the focus. Self was the new god, and humankind's opinions and feelings had become the new "truth."

The third chapter of Genesis is one of the most important chapters in the Bible. If our view of this chapter is inaccurate, then it is highly probable that our view of the rest of Scripture is distorted. This chapter exposes the universal human problem of sin. Humanity inherited sin from the first Adam, thereby setting the stage for our Savior and Redeemer, the second Adam. The apostle Paul teaches this truth in his epistle to the Romans: "When Adam sinned, sin entered the world. Adam's sin brought death, so death spread to everyone, for everyone sinned" (5:12 NLT).

Genesis chapter three identifies the problem of sin when the eyes of both Adam and Eve were opened and they reached out to become like God, wanting to know good and evil. The answer to the problem of sin is the New Testament gospel: the death, burial, and resurrection of the Lord Jesus Christ, the sacrificial Lamb who became humankind's penalty for sin. Paul in Romans expounds on this further:

> Still, everyone died—from the time of Adam to the time of Moses—even those who did not disobey an explicit commandment of God, as Adam did. Now Adam is a symbol, a representation of Christ, who was yet to come. But there is a great difference between Adam's sin and God's

gracious gift. For the sin of this one man, Adam, brought death to many. But even greater is God's wonderful grace and his gift of forgiveness to many through this other man, Jesus Christ. And the result of God's gracious gift is very different from the result of that one man's sin. For Adam's sin led to condemnation, but God's free gift leads to our being made right with God, even though we are guilty of many sins. For the sin of this one man, Adam, caused death to rule over many. But even greater is God's wonderful grace and his gift of righteousness, for all who receive it will live in triumph over sin and death through this one man, Jesus Christ. Yes, Adam's one sin brings condemnation for everyone, but Christ's one act of righteousness brings a right relationship with God and new life for everyone. Because one person disobeyed God, many became sinners. But because one other person obeyed God, many will be made righteous. God's law was given so that all people could see how sinful they were. But as people sinned more and more, God's wonderful grace became more abundant. So just as sin ruled over all people and brought them to death, now God's wonderful grace rules instead, giving us right standing with God and resulting in eternal life through Jesus Christ our Lord (Romans 5:14–21 NLT).

What God had created good became perverse. Will and desire led the first man and woman to disobey the Lord God. Who influenced them to rebel against the ways of God? The arch nemesis of God's creation, Satan, who used against Adam and Eve the same thing he had used to entice a third of the angels to follow him from heaven: deception. And those under deception are the last ones to believe they are being deceived. Spiritual deception is when Satan works on the mind to get us to see circumstances, ourselves, and life in general from his point of view. And whenever his point of view matches something in our heart, destruction awaits.

Jesus Speaks About Deception

Jesus spoke about deception frequently, and especially concerning the last days:

> Later, Jesus sat on the Mount of Olives. His disciples came to him privately and said, "Tell us, when will all this happen? What sign will signal your return and the end of the world?" Jesus told them, "Don't let anyone mislead you, for many will come in my name, claiming, 'I am the Messiah.' They will deceive many. And you will hear of wars and threats of wars, but don't panic. Yes, these things must take place, but the end won't follow immediately. Nation will go to war against nation, and kingdom against kingdom. There will be famines and earthquakes in many parts of the world. But all this is only the first of the birth pains, with more to come. Then you will be arrested, persecuted, and killed. You will be hated all over the world because you are my followers. And many will turn away from me and betray and hate each other. And many false prophets will appear and will deceive many people. Sin will be rampant everywhere, and the love of many will grow cold. But the one who endures to the end will be saved. And the Good News about the Kingdom will be preached throughout the whole world, so that all nations will hear it; and then the end will come" (Matthew 24: 3–14 NLT).

Jesus referenced wars, famines, and earthquakes, but the first thing he mentioned regarding the signal of his return and the end of the world was deception. "Jesus told them, 'Don't let anyone mislead you, for many will come in my name, claiming, 'I am the Messiah.' They will deceive many." Today's church is suffering from the very thing Christ warned us about. Deception runs rampant throughout the body of Christ. It doesn't matter what denomination we attend or what side of the "persuasion" fence we sit on. Deception has intensified.

Self-aggrandizement, social media fame, and a desire to be validated has helped flame this destructive fire. Jesus warned his followers: "Then if anyone tells you, 'Look, here is the Messiah,' or 'There he is,' don't believe it. For false messiahs and false prophets will rise up and perform great signs and wonders so as to deceive, if possible, even God's chosen ones. See, I have warned you about this ahead of time" (Matthew 24:23–25 NLT).

Jesus spoke about deception four times more than any other subject in the New Testament. Why? Because being deceived is a reality; absolutely no one is exempt. Does the Garden of Eden have anything to do with this? The apostle Paul seemed to think so in his warning to the church in Corinth:

> I hope you will put up with me in a little foolishness. Yes, please put up with me! I am jealous for you with a godly jealousy. I promised you to one husband, to Christ, so that I might present you as a pure virgin to him. But I am afraid that just as Eve was deceived by the serpent's cunning, your minds may somehow be led astray from your sincere and pure devotion to Christ. For if someone comes to you and preaches a Jesus other than the Jesus we preached, or if you receive a different spirit from the Spirit you received, or a different gospel from the one you accepted, you put up with it easily enough (2 Corinthians 11:1–4 NIV).

What happened in the Garden is not just a story; it is real history. It is an established truth for the present and a stern prophetic warning for the future. That is why I have written this book—to awaken the church to the danger of our times. Many books are available about defending our faith from external attacks; this book is about defending our faith from internal attacks. To be effective in defending the church from within we have to shatter the idols and inverted beliefs that have been erected in the house of God. The winds of post-truth have blown in a corrupt and unbiblical view that to speak against the tenor of the times is unhealthy, critical, irrelevant, negative, overly harsh, condemning, and unloving. Paul himself was a recipient of this very backlash when he evidenced concern about the believers in Galatia being bewitched by deception:

> You did not mistreat me when I first preached to you. Surely you remember that I was sick when I first brought you the Good News. But even though my condition tempted you to reject me, you did not despise me or turn me away. No, you took me in and cared for me as though I were an angel from God or even Christ Jesus himself. Where is that joyful and grateful spirit you felt then? I am sure you would have taken out your own eyes and given them to me if it had been possible. Have I now become your enemy because I am telling you the truth? Those false teachers are so eager to win your favor, but their intentions are not good. They are trying to shut you off from me so that you will pay attention only to them (Galatians 4:12-17 NLT).

This is the power of deception working on people who once had a fruitful relationship with Christ but who now are deceived. Under the influence of deception the right thing appears wrong, and the wrong thing appears right. Satan has bewitched many in the church to ridicule and magnify the "strictness" of God while de-emphasizing the seriousness of his warnings. If God had to warn Adam and Eve while they were in their state of innocence, what does that say about us who are born with a sinful nature? This book is a prophetic warning to believers. One Greek word for warning is *noutheto*, meaning to impart understanding or to put pressure on the mind in order to exert influence upon one's will, desires, and decisions with the intention of guiding and pointing in a right direction. My desire is to point readers back to the lordship of Christ, who is the head of the church.

Our Adversary has planted many landmines among us. My prayer is that this book not only help uncover the deadly landmines (deception) but also help recover our passion for historical biblical truths and produce in us true conformity to Christ.

THE PREP COURSE

We live in a world filled with danger, and because of that, warnings are necessary for survival. They protect and preserve those who obey. Romans 15:4 assures us: "For whatever things were written before were written for our learning, that we through the patience and comfort of the Scriptures might have hope." The Word of God is filled with instructions, decrees, and warnings. Without them, how would we be able to live the life God desires us to live?

Let us consider Abraham and Sarah. In Genesis chapter sixteen we read of the consequences of their impatience. Abraham had been promised by God that he would have a male child. After ten years and still no baby, they took it upon themselves to try and "help" God: "Now Sarai, Abram's wife, had borne him no children. But she had an Egyptian slave named Hagar; so she said to Abram, 'The LORD has kept me from having children. Go, sleep with my slave; perhaps I can build a family through her.' Abram agreed to what Sarai said" (v. 1–2). This ungodly agreement went very wrong, producing a son named Ishmael, whose descendants have been enemies of the Jews for centuries. Being led by the flesh is a serious hazard to spiritual growth.

Picture yourself on a flight to God's destination for your life. The flight is long, but you have no worries because you recognize who is controlling the plane, and you trust him to get you there. Then, all of a sudden, a passenger begins to act out. He is fed up with the lengthy flight and insists that the pilot hurry up and get to the destination. Flight attendants are doing their best to deal with him, but he refuses to be tamed and demands that his needs be met. The passenger's actions worsen to outright disrespect, even violence. The pilot is forced to make an emergency landing, which affects every single passenger on board. You are furious because this unruly passenger's insubordination has caused everyone to be late to their destination.

The rebellious, wild passenger is our flesh, and the in-flight staff the passenger disrespected is the Holy Spirit. That which is born of the flesh will never seek to comply; it looks to control! The flesh is dangerous, and we must beware of its capabilities. The Evil One seeks to influence us to act out in our flesh against God so that we can actually miss his will for our lives.

The Knowledge of God

> Therefore I also, after I heard of your faith in the Lord Jesus and your love for all the saints, do not cease to give thanks for you, making mention of you in my prayers: that the God of our Lord Jesus Christ, the Father of glory, may give to you the spirit of wisdom and revelation in the knowledge of Him, the eyes of your understanding being enlightened; that you may know what is the hope of his calling, what are the riches of the glory of his inheritance in the saints" (Ephesians 1:15–18).

The apostle Paul prayed that the people would grow in the knowledge of God. This knowledge is not just intellectual head knowledge, which in the Greek is *gnosis*. It is not reading a book about God and saying, "I now know who God is." Instead, the knowledge of God comes through an encounter, experience, or difficulty. For this Paul uses the word *epignosis*, knowledge that not only stimulates intellectual understanding but also transforms one's character and influences the heart into full surrender. This spirit of wisdom that Paul wanted us to receive enables us to perceive accurately. We should think of the spirit of wisdom as the ability to apply the knowledge of God—spiritual truths—in life's situations.

If we could use our intellect to make it through life and actually succeed in doing so, Paul would not have had to pray for believers. That he does pray for us demonstrates the importance of wisdom and insight.

Unlike disciples who were taught in person by Christ while he was on earth, the apostle Paul was taught by him while he (Christ) was exalted in his heavenly position. This means Paul received heavenly revelation in order to contribute to the New Testament. Paul prayed for us because the very thing we need to navigate life has to be revealed to us. Believers cannot understand or apply God's will unless God, by his Spirit, exposes or reveals it to us.

FOR GREATER UNDERSTANDING

Revelation *means "to unveil something hidden" or "to bring insight to a spiritual truth heretofore covered up." Revelation is something hidden in Scripture and revealed by God whose meaning will never compete with or fall outside of the Word of God. In other words, God will never reveal something that contradicts what is in the Bible. God does not hand out hidden truths to just anyone though; there is a price we must pay in order to receive a revelation from God. For example, before he received a revealed truth, the prophet Daniel went to the lion's den. John was in prison on an island for criminals, sent there to be tortured. God was preparing John and Daniel for a revelation.*

Fables and Wives' Tales

Some things we believe are false. We have heard them for so long that we assume they are true. Popular culture calls these beliefs urban legends. An urban legend is a commonly circulated view repeated throughout the culture and down through the ages as something that is valid when in fact it is not true. Many false and unreliable teachings have been passed down in the church, and we believe them without question. In his pastoral epistles addressed to Timothy and Titus, Paul warned them not to accept these fables and wives' tales:

> As I urged you when I went to Macedonia—remain in Ephesus that you may charge some that they teach no other doctrine, nor give heed to fables and endless genealogies, which cause disputes rather than godly edification which is in faith (1 Timothy 1:3–4).

> If you instruct the brethren on these things, you will be a good minister of Jesus Christ, nourished in the words of faith and of the good doctrine which you have carefully followed. But reject profane and old wives' fables, and exercise yourself toward godliness (1 Timothy 4:6–7).

> For the time will come when they will not endure sound doctrine, but according to their own desires, because they have itchy ears, they will heap up for themselves teachers; and they will turn their ears away from the truth, and be turned aside to fables (2 Timothy 4:3–4).

> This testimony is true. Therefore rebuke them sharply, that they may be sound in the faith, not giving heed to Jewish fables and commandments of men who turn from the truth (Titus 1:13–14).

The Greek word for fables is *mythos,* fanciful and fictional stories fabricated by the undisciplined mind. In essence, a fable is a falsehood. And one of the lies passed down in our time is that we as true believers cannot be deceived.

What Does the Text Actually Say?

When readers impose their own interpretations or views into a text, they are doing *eisegesis,* which is interpreting a text by reading *into it* one's own biases rather than reading what the text actually says. When this happens, one's particular views lead the text instead of the text leading the individual. The objective in eisegesis is not to discover the author's intent of a verse but to use the verse to serve one's position. We see this frequently in the church today where people are consistently injecting their presuppositions into the Scriptures. Jesus never approved of that sort of reading of Scripture. Paul explains in 2 Thessalonians 2:9–10 that "the coming of the lawless one will be in accordance with how Satan works. He will use all sorts of displays of power through signs and wonders that serve the lie, and all the ways that wickedness deceives those who are perishing. They perish because they refused to love the truth and so be saved." When we misread Scripture, we do the work of Satan, who uses every kind of evil deception to fool those on their way to destruction.

This warning goes all the way back to the first man and woman in the Garden of Eden. Because there was no obedience to revealed truth, Adam and Eve, who were made without sin, became casualties.

No person on earth is safe from Satan's deception. Christians are never to read their own intentions into the Bible; they are to examine the clear meaning of Scripture and critically interpret it in its correct context, which also includes correlation of the text—how does this passage relate to the rest of Scripture.

Even the Elect Can Be Deceived

The terms *elect* and *election* have been misrepresented and abused in our day, and because of this, deception and pride have taken root in the lives of many within the body of Christ. One particular verse taken out of its context has led to some of the confusion. In Matthew 24:24, Jesus said, "For false christs and false prophets will rise and show great signs and wonders to deceive, if possible, even the elect." The word *elect* as used in the Bible is not an individual term but a corporate one. Isaiah 45:4 reads, "For Jacob my servant's sake, and Israel mine elect." A single person is not elect, but a group. And Romans 9:6 tells us that it is the nation of Israel, not merely someone of Jewish descent, who is elect (chosen). The apostle Peter wrote: "But you are a chosen generation, a royal priesthood, a holy nation, his own special people . . . ." (1 Peter 2:9). Individuals in the body of Christ are not elect; their election is as part of the entire church. Because of an incorrect understanding of *elect*, many wrongly believe they cannot be deceived. But is this actually what Jesus was saying? No. Keep in mind who Jesus was speaking to and what he said earlier in that chapter. He was speaking to the apostles, chosen by him, and the first warning sign he told them to be aware of was deception. They questioned him:

> "....Tell us, when will all this happen? What sign will signal your return, and the end of the world?" Jesus told them, "Don't let anyone mislead you...." (Matthew 24:3–4 NLT).

Why would Jesus warn of something that couldn't possibly happen? The reading of our own opinions into Matthew 24:24 has led some Christians to erroneously believe they are immune to Satan's deception. (Reading any verse through the lens of one's own viewpoint is dangerous! *Exegesis*, which is reading the true meaning *out of* rather than into Scripture—without bias even from our favorite spiritual leaders—requires disallowing any personal interpretation that does not arise out of what the Scripture actually says.) If we read Matthew 24 through a correct lens, we see that Christ was not emphasizing whether the elect can or cannot be deceived; he was stressing the point that deception can be so believable and attractive that even the elect (an entire group) can be fooled. Again, the Lord was not speaking in reference to individuals but to an entire group. The late New Testament scholar F. F. Bruce cited that "forty-seven percent of the New Testament deals with the defending and contending of our faith." Why would nearly half of the New Testament be about contending for the faith if believers cannot be deceived? We as believers can be deceived. (Have we forgotten the reason we are all born into sin? Is it not because our first parents who, *even though they were without a sin nature,* were deceived?!)

- If we think our love for God will prevent us from being deceived then we have already been deceived.
- If we think we can create a Christian utopia where we will not be harassed by Satan then we are greatly deceived.
- If we think that being in a church that preaches sound doctrine makes us immune to Satan's deception then sadly, we are being extremely deceived.

There is no place on earth where we are untouchable by Satan. How can we put limits on the god of this world? If Satan can walk in a Garden that was perfectly created by God then everything on earth is at his disposal.

The god of this world is an imitator of the true God. Martin Luther said, "Whenever God builds a church, Satan builds a chapel next door." Satan is drawn to anything God has his name on. If God's name is on your church, job, marriage, or anything else, you can be sure Satan will be drawn there.

It is important to keep in mind that just because Satan shows up does not mean we should let him stay. If we respond correctly, his visit will be short-lived, but there are many who will unwittingly invite the Evil One to live in their guest bedroom. And if he has already moved into our guest bedroom, it is because we have moved away from God.

God Departs and Satan Comes In

Satan dominates those who outwardly express confessions of faith but inwardly experience no change. Even if one is of the household of faith but repeatedly rejects warnings, God will move out since he is not wanted. When this happens, one will see evidence that Satan moves in and takes over. The first sign is that there will be a lack of honoring God's ways—a lack of illumination of the Word of God—because the Holy Spirit is no longer there to bring clarification. This happened in the days of Eli, the High Priest. Because of the sins of Eli and his sons, it was written: "In those days the word of the LORD was rare; there were not many visions" (1 Samuel 3:1). The word *rare* in Hebrew means something that's precious or valuable. The deceitfulness of sin had led to the hardness of heart among the people and their leaders, and this caused divine revelation to be limited. Whenever sin dominates, the true Word of God deteriorates!

Next, there is no "word in due season" (Proverbs 15:23). This means that someone can teach something intellectually correct and yet it have no positive effect spiritually because the Holy Spirit is nowhere to be found. A word in due season is influenced only by the Holy Spirit. Isaiah wrote: "The Lord God has given me the tongue of the learned, that I should know how to speak a word in season to him who is weary. He awakens me morning by morning, he awakens my ear to hear as the learned" (50:4). King Solomon penned: "A man has joy by the answer of his mouth, And a word spoken in due season, how good it is!" (Proverbs 15:23).

No one who remains in habitual sin should expect God to move. Nor should he expect that an authentic spiritual gift would function as it was intended. Someone may say, But the gifts and the calling come without repentance! That is another misuse of a biblical passage. Paul's statement in Romans 11 that the gifts and the calling of God are irrevocable was not a reference to the gifts of the Spirit but to God's election of the nation of Israel. In essence, Paul was stating that even though Israel had rejected Christ, he had not totally forsaken her. He would be faithful in keeping his promise to Abraham (Genesis 17:7). The Holy Spirit governs spiritual gifts, and they are not distributed to those who have not accepted Christ in faith and who are not living consistently in faith.

True Contentment

Did you know Satan can live in a church where there is consistent rejection of previous warnings? And when Satan takes over a church, there will be a marked increase in adding and subtracting from the Word of God. When this happens, a person can no longer see Christ. Where there is no revelation, people start living loosely, as though life cannot be governed.

When Satan governs the mind, we become fiercely independent. Exodus 32 provides a perfect illustration of what happens. After the nation of Israel was rescued from Egypt, Moses headed for Mount Sinai to receive instructions from God. The Israelites grew impatient waiting for him to return and decided to try and secure God's presence by surrounding Aaron and requesting that he make them gods who could lead them (Exodus 32:1). Instead of Aaron restraining the people until Moses returned, he gave in and called for the people to bring him all their gold. He melted it down, molded it into the shape of a calf, and even created an altar for this false god. On that very day, judgment broke out because the people had turned away from God's laws.

There must be a redemptive word from God revealed to us in order to govern the way we live. Proverbs 29:18 says: "When people do not accept divine guidance, they run wild. But whoever obeys the law is joyful" (NLT). When the Word of God governs the life of believers, there is true contentment. Contentment means that one is fully satisfied inwardly to the exclusion of external circumstances. This kind of contentment comes by obeying God's Word. It eliminates the notion that we can be happy because of what we obtain. Even when experiencing great turmoil, we respect the Word of God, and we live by it. When we truly live by the Word, we realize that everything in life can be wrong and still we will have contentment and peace. That is a condition of the heart and nothing else.

The Clearer Things Are, the Stronger the Deception

We saw it with Adam and Eve, and we see it in churches today: people resist submitting to anything or anyone who doesn't support or reaffirm the autonomy of their will. They know what they are doing is wrong, but they do it anyway. When Christians disobey, spiritual outcomes are never good (Romans 1:18–19). Thankfully, God in his mercy reveals his truths to us so we can respond the way he wants us to. A simple but potent warning, however, is that as God reveals more, Satan becomes more aggressive; the clearer things are, the stronger deception becomes.

God does not allow Satan to test us unless he's sure we are equipped to overcome. God ultimately controls the limit of Satan's opposition. Satan visiting us can result in a good thing or a bad thing; it all depends on how we respond. Victorious finishes depend on what we do with the help God gives us. We see this in the life of Job. After being touched by Satan and confronted by God, Job recognized God's sovereignty and received a great ending (Job 42).

Three aspects of the inner self that must be intact for us to have a favorable end are:

- We must be biblically grounded both emotionally and mentally;
- We must not be controlled by emotional impulses;
- We must have stable minds.

We should not overthink our strength in these areas, for pride will ignite the attacks of Satan. He is crafty and knows not to attack in an obvious way. Often when he comes around, he will use someone we are comfortable with. One might not open their door to someone unknown but will leave the door unlocked for someone considered a close friend. The god of this world does not play fair; he must never be underestimated (Jude 1:8–10). Satan gets to us through our weakest areas, and if he knows we are moved by impulses, he will push our buttons. If our thoughts are not harnessed, he will have them all over the place. Satan is an expert when it comes to mind games.

Much like a suave salesperson who skillfully pitches the benefits of a product, Satan does not force us but persuades us to act (1 Chronicles 21:1–14). His greatest weapon is his words. Satan does more damage talking than afflicting, and deception has led more astray than persecution has. This is precisely where we find the beginning of the fall of man—with Eve allowing the Serpent's deceptive words to push her into disobeying God.

It is foolish and immature to decide things while the mind is cloudy and when God's perspective is not sought. God wants us to have biblical discernment—the ability to sift through and sort out things that do not line up with his point of view and to distinguish right from wrong.

God Wants Us to Have Biblical Discernment

Through trials and temptations God has a way of getting us to a place we would never have reached had Satan not visited us. Jesus grew in strength after Satan left him. He held his ground and fought with the right words in the right context (Luke 4:1–14). There are many profound truths in the biblical account of Jesus' temptations. One in particular is that in his humanity, not his divinity, Jesus overcame Satan. He became the example of how we too can be victorious in difficult times.

When Satan visits us, we are tempted to be depressed, confused, and emotional and to refuse to do what we ought to do. How long he stays, how long we remain in a trial, and how well things turn out all go back to how much we truly love and trust and obey God.

Paterology is the doctrine of God as Father. In the Garden Eve questioned God's ability to be a good father. Her thought process was something like, "If you are a good father, then why are you holding things back from me? Why are you keeping me from enjoying something that doesn't look at all evil?" (Of course, this is the Serpent talking. When he shows up in believers' lives, he always has an objective, and that is to cause us to dishonor God's character and to disrespect his words.) Eve's theology was shaped by perceived rejection, and this caused her to feel hurt. She was more interested in felt experience than a faith experience.

When people lose patience and try being happy on their own, they usually see no harm in what they are doing. But when we make premature decisions, we move ourselves from where God planted us in our quest to discover relief. Let me ask you: When was the gospel ever about God making us happy? For the sake of happiness, have we forsaken what the New Testament really teaches? Have we forgotten about denying self and taking up our cross daily?

In the Garden it was Adam that Satan really wanted, but he thought that if he went through Eve he could cause them both to stumble. He thought that perhaps when Adam saw that the woman did not die when she took something God told her they could not have, they both would come to doubt and disrespect God's Word. Brothers and sisters, in dealing with us Satan wants to take down as many as possible. If we're not careful, we can easily go from offending God to misleading others because of our self-centered view of him. We must make sure we are submissive to Christ in order to give others the right advice.

When Satan threatens our lives, we can remember these lessons from the Garden:

- We must discern that Satan is here since we can't fight what we cannot see.
- We must discern who Satan is speaking through because he likes to come through people we are most comfortable with.
- We must discern his objective for coming because this will help us govern ourselves rightly.
- We must go into self-examination mode to make sure there is nothing in us that he will be drawn to. Satan is easily drawn to lust, anger, pride, discontentment, covetousness, envy, unforgiveness, rejection, doubt (which deals with our view of God), and unbelief (which deals with what God says).

God wants us to rightly handle what he shows us, so we must discern. We cannot receive things from God if we have a wrong view of him.

The Pathology of a Lie

A lot of believers are victims of the Serpent. Many have moved away from God through deception, becoming targets for disobedience and trickery. But God wants to teach us not to be deceived by the Serpent's schemes.

Pathology studies the nature of disease and its causes, process, development, and consequences. Through examination and experiment pathologists study to understand how once healthy bodies become damaged. For example, if cancer is involved in the death of a person, a pathologist will cut out a piece of human tissue and send it to a laboratory to be examined.

Well, we must become spiritual pathologists when being fed lies from the Evil One. Satan's intention is always to lie, but his lies do not appear to be lies. Satan does not show up as an angel of darkness but an angel of light! If we misunderstand the process and development of a lie, there will be consequences. Remember, Satan caused a lie to prevail even in heaven! He fashioned a lie in the most perfect environment, causing one-third of heaven's angels to stumble (Revelation 12:4). The angel whom God once called Lucifer, the Son of the Morning, turned on him and became the Devil. God changed

Lucifer's name to Satan, which means "adversary" or "accuser." This was for our benefit, so humans would know how he works.

Satan will visit us—either externally through people or circumstances, or internally through our thoughts—but however he shows up, it is important that we know he is there because his strength comes from being undetected. This is why we see nations spending billions of dollars on stealth technology: you can't fight or defeat what you cannot see! So be warned: the Devil will never announce his arrival; rather, he will appear as an angel of light (2 Corinthians 11:13–15). Therefore, we must recognize first that Satan is present. Then we must know

- who he is using;
- what circumstances he is using;
- what his objective is in coming; and
- how God wants us to respond.

External and Internal Signs of Satan's Presence

An external sign of Satan's presence is that he brings someone into our lives who is dishonest—someone who will lie to us or about us. An internal sign is that our minds become consumed with lies and confusion. These lies can range from suicidal thoughts to a changed view concerning God and his church. No mind is safe from Satan's wiles of deception. This internal attack on the mind is a type of spiritual warfare in which Satan convinces us to see things from his point of view. He wraps his lies comfortably within our own mindset and feelings making them seem to be true.

What can help us win in spiritual warfare? Certainly not street smarts! We are no match for the craftiness of Satan, and we cannot outthink him. For the weapons of our warfare are not through carnal or fleshy means but mighty through God (2 Corinthians 10:4). In fact, trying to best the Enemy shows we are deceived already. If we are not able to control tomorrow, what makes us think we can outsmart a supernatural being? If Satan could convince the angels in heaven there was something wrong about God's character, he will certainly be able to convince us. What could he tell an angel, who was created by God and saw him every day, that would convince the angel to leave heaven? Those angels would not have departed unless they bought into Satan's argument that God had flaws.

Satan will convince us that we are correctly discerning a matter only to lead us to a very negative consequence. In a mere one-time encounter with Eve, Satan used persuasion in order to convince. When he visits us, it is not just to have conversation. No, he wants to move us out of the will of God, and he will argue and convince until his will is done.

It was in prison where the apostle Paul wrote a letter to the Colossian church urging them to watch out for damaging doctrines that were invading the church. Paul began by commending them for their response to the Good News and for their love for the saints. They knew the gospel was true because it had changed their lives.

In Colossians 1:9, Paul writes: "For this reason, since the day we heard about you, we have not stopped praying for you. We continually ask God to fill you with the knowledge of his will through all the wisdom and understanding that the Spirit gives." The apostle does not ask the Colossians to obtain intellectual knowledge but rather knowledge that comes through submission to the truth. To understand God's viewpoint requires submission of the heart. We cannot know God's will when the heart does not desire to surrender to it (John 7:16–18).

Paul continually asked God to fill the Colossians with the knowledge of his will. The word *fill* in this context means being fully possessed and dominated—filled to the brim. When we are possessed by God in this way, we will be filled with spiritual wisdom and understanding and live lives pleasing to God.

Satan Meets Us with Lies

Most of us will never know how fully our hearts are surrendered to God until we are placed in situations not of our choosing. In a heart not fully surrendered there may rise up pride, frustration, and rebellion, but God wants us to take delight in the situations we find ourselves because it is he who puts us there (James 1:1–16). In the twentieth chapter of the book of Acts, Paul says that everywhere he went, chains waited for him. "I only know that in every city the Holy Spirit warns me that prison and hardships are facing me" (20:23). Paul was not disconcerted by this because he did not count his life dear to himself. Rather, he endured the struggle so his relationship would be perfect with God.

When we desire a perfect relationship with God, that's when Satan comes around. He does not want us to grow or reach maturity in Christ. He shows up when he knows God is trying to mature us. He does not want us to have the relationship with God that he could never have again.

Jesus modeled for us the right response whenever the Serpent arrives to do what he does best. After God identified Jesus, "Then Jesus was led by the Spirit into the wilderness to be tempted by the devil" (Matthew 4:1). He will meet us with similar lies after God reveals something to us. If God does not speak, then what is the point of Satan tempting us? But the fact that God does speak shows that even Satan must believe what God says. Satan taunted Jesus while he was hungry to turn stones into bread if he was the Son of God (Matthew 4:3). Satan knew who Jesus was, but he was trying to get him to prove himself while in a weak position. He was hoping Jesus would use his power to meet his own needs. Had Jesus moved independently of the Father, the whole test would be violated. It was a high-level, strategic game.

Satan attacked Jesus with strategic questions while Jesus was vulnerable. The Tempter heard what God had said (Matthew 3:17) and repeated the same thing to Jesus in trying to deceive him. This was the very thing he did with Eve. Remember, our God has no rival, but the people made in his image do. If Satan wants to reach God, he will come through God's people with deception on his lips.

The Dragon, the Devil, and Diablos

We know of Satan's former position and how he currently functions, but who is he? He is our adversary, our opponent, who is continually hostile towards us. When Satan is being himself, his purpose is to resist us. In the book of Revelation, chapter twelve, he appears as an enormous red dragon with seven heads, ten horns, and seven crowns on its heads. The dragon represents persecution. Satan did not show up in the Garden of Eden as a dragon. He knew he could not persecute Adam and Eve because they were without sin. Instead, he got them with deception, the tool that had worked for him in heaven.

Another way Satan approaches us is as the Devil. The word *devil* is the translation of "diablos," from which we get the English term "false accuser" or "slanderer." When Satan is the Devil, his objective is to use slander. A slanderer is one who utters false charges or misrepresentations designed to damage one's reputation. Satan wants us to be either victims of slander or carriers of slander.

When Diablos isn't slandering someone, he is causing backbiting. This is when someone makes malicious comments about a person who is not present to defend himself or herself. Satan's presence can be detected whenever we see him using someone in this way. Satan knows what excites our temper and what hurts us most. When we are vulnerable, Satan allows us to hear false statements uttered on purpose—lying, slandering, and backbiting.

Satan understood from the outset that he could not shock Eve with a lie. He would have to get familiar with her and appear as someone with reliable information, taking what she knew and adding his own twist to it—deception. The apostle Paul understood the dangers of deception. In 2 Corinthians 11, Paul wrote: "I fear that somehow your pure and undivided devotion to Christ will be corrupted, just as Eve was deceived by the cunning ways of the serpent" (NLT). To *deceive* means to persuade someone through false promises to get them to be disobedient. *Cunning* means craftiness—clever manipulation designed to look like truth. One who is cunning, or crafty, will be willing to do or say anything to achieve the goal of deception.

WARNING

The Mosaic Law to which Jews ascribed had a system in place designed to provide legitimacy in finding a man guilty (Deuteronomy 19:15). It's why when Jesus was on trial, at least two witnesses were required for him to be found guilty and sentenced to death. Matthew 26:59–60 says, "The chief priests and the whole Sanhedrin were looking for false evidence against Jesus so that they could put him to death, but found none. Even though many false witnesses came forward, they found none." The Scripture continues, "But at last two false witnesses came forward and said, "This fellow said, 'I am able to destroy the temple of God and to build it in three days (vs. 60–61).'"

The Greek word for a lie is pseudos. It is used to describe statements intended to deceive. Someone who tries to deceive knows a thing is not true but repeats the untruth in order to mislead. Satan is the Father of Lies. He used deception to accelerate Jesus' death. He used false witnesses to get Jesus killed. False witnesses take bits and pieces of information and create false narratives to support a given position. They provide partial truths to a plausible argument, but the whole purpose of their testimony is to persuade listeners that what is being said is real.

> *A lie will take off at top speed. The truth moves slowly, but in the final analysis, truth will prevail. This is why at times God does not want his followers to defend themselves but rather to endure. The way to defeat a lie is to remain surrendered to truth. God cannot and will not associate with a lie. To do so would go against his very nature. "God is not human, that he should lie" (Numbers 23:19).*
>
> *In Proverbs chapter six, we learn that a lying tongue and a false witness are among the seven things God hates: "There are six things the Lord hates, seven that are detestable to him: haughty eyes, a **lying tongue**, hands that shed innocent blood, a heart that devises wicked schemes, feet that are quick to rush into evil, a **false witness who pours out lies** and a person who stirs up conflict in the community" (vs. 16–19 NIV, emphasis added).*
>
> *Many Bible scholars believe whenever a numerical list is given in Hebrew, it is ordered from least to greatest. If this is true, notice that this list begins with pride and ends with lies and discord. Sounds a whole lot like Lucifer and his rebellion in heaven, doesn't it?*
>
> *A false witness who pours out lies will not go unpunished because a false witness works for Satan. A constant liar is considered a worthless and wicked person, a troublemaker and a villain, who goes about with a corrupt mouth (Proverbs 6:12). They do things to get attention, always stirring up trouble. Their actions will lead to their destruction.*

When the Serpent Speaks

It may be easy to tell when another person is lying, but it is not easy to tell when the Serpent is speaking deception into our thoughts. Satan knew he could not approach Adam by himself without help from Eve. (It is hard to deceive a man who talks face to face with God.) His strategic plan was to wait until Adam was occupied to approach Eve. Once Eve ate of the tree, the book of Genesis never mentions the Serpent again. Perhaps he knew Eve would be a carrier of his lie. When she finally ate the fruit in front of Adam and did not die—after

God had said, "You shall not eat, for in the day that you eat of it you shall surely die" (Genesis 2:17)—Adam also disobeyed God and ate.

Satan has been afflicting people through others for a very long time. Everything he does is strategic, aimed at tendencies we all have. If Satan knows you are finished doing things God's way, he will leave you alone, but if your desire is to keep the commandments of God, you can be certain that Satan will come to make war with you.

Only the Truth Will Set Us Free

Satan deceived the whole world (1 John 5:19). Consequently, the whole world is under his persuasion because of a lie. When the Enemy wants to deceive us, he will throw lies our way. In the eighth chapter of his gospel, John writes, "To the Jews who believed him, Jesus said, 'If you hold to my teaching, you are really my disciples. Then you will know the truth, and the truth will set you free'" (8:31–32 NIV). But the people claimed they had never been in bondage to anyone. Keep in mind, they were in bondage in Egypt for four hundred years, and they were in bondage in Babylon for seventy years! People influenced by a lying spirit cannot tolerate the truth.

Under the persuasion of a lie, even great zeal can blind us from truth (Acts 26:1–18). This is why Paul's encounter on the road to Damascus in Acts 9 was so dramatic. Paul, a zealot, was so entrenched in a lie that he thought he was working for God when in reality he was working for Satan. It took hearing Jesus' voice in a most dramatic way for Paul to be rescued from the lie that had entangled him. Raised by Pharisees, Paul had approved of Christians being killed. He was zealous in that which he thought was right (Acts 22:1–5). But it took only one encounter with the Lord to get Paul on the right track. When we are deceived, God may do things supernaturally to bring us out from under the lie that holds us captive. Paul's story teaches that while a lie will have us thinking God needs us, once we get truth, we see how much we need God.

Coming Out of a Lie

The word *lie* is associated with deception because the objective of a lie is to deceive. The purpose of the lie is to cauterize one's ability to respond to truth. That is why every time we believe a lie or walk in a lie, it is harder to accept the truth. And if we cannot respond to truth, we cannot respond to the Holy Spirit. Jesus told us that if we hold to his teaching, "Then you will know the truth, and the truth will set you free" (John 8:31–32).

In order to be set free, we must first acknowledge that a lie is holding us captive. This is most difficult for those struggling with pride. Secondly, if we know something is wrong, we must not stay in it. Though sin brings temporary pleasure, it leads to death for all who partake in it (Hebrews 11:23–27). God is merciful, and he will rescue them who choose to obey. The only way to defeat a lie is by remaining surrendered to the truth.

The Ploy

We have gone through the prep course and examined the origin of lies; now we examine the Enemy's strategy. A *ploy* is a calculated, cunning scheme to get someone to do something in order to obtain an advantage over him. Satan's ploys cause people to lose what they were never supposed to lose. His attempts to turn others to his evil cause should never be underestimated.

Satan and a third of the angels were kicked out of heaven when Satan's plan to become equal with the one true God failed (Isaiah 14:12–15). Now he will never again have the chance to spend eternity with God. Satan already knows his destination (Revelation 20:10). He does not want man to enjoy God's presence for all eternity, which is why he is bent on deceiving us.

Satan's Ploy Comes Through the Familiar

How did Satan move Adam and Eve off course? Well, Satan is very calculating in whom he chooses and how he uses. He knew that Adam's job was to cultivate the Garden, so he waited until Adam was cultivating to approach Eve. (Someone had to be the pawn in Satan's hand.) Eve would be a conduit to capture Adam. He would speak to her with a silver tongue through a created being with which she was familiar. (At one point serpents must have had the ability to speak.) While we might run in the opposite direction if a serpent spoke to us, for Eve a talking serpent was nothing out of the ordinary. Satan had to use something familiar to Eve in order for his plan to succeed. He tricked Eve, and then once he got through to Adam, he indirectly challenged God.

We can see a similar betrayal with Judas and Jesus. Satan used someone familiar to Jesus to betray him. Another example is Job's wife, who told Job to "Curse God and die" (Job 2:9). Satan uses people like puppets; he cares nothing about them. His agenda is to get to God by causing that which he created to disobey him. His ploy is to make sure we hear God's command but act as if we do not know God. We must guard against becoming victims of the Serpent by listening to what is false from the mouths of people close to us. The Serpent pollutes our minds by making friendly conversations hard to discern. If we're not careful, we find ourselves making decisions, reacting, and responding in ways we will later regret. The reason for our confusion and regret is that in reality we are conversing not with a trusted friend but with a serpent. We cannot think our minds will remain sober if we have consistent conversation with the Serpent!

Genesis 3:1 reads that "The serpent was more cunning than any beast in the field that God had made." In the original Hebrew language, the term for cunning is *aruwm*. It means wise, shrewd, or crafty. Satan picked the animal that appeared the wisest to push his agenda forward. And because his plan prevailed, it caused the serpent to become the most cursed of any animal: "So the Lord God said to the serpent, 'Because you have done this, cursed are you above all livestock and all wild animals! You will crawl on your belly and you will eat dust all the days of your life'" (Genesis 3:14). Snakes—and people too—will pay a price when used by Satan.

Eve questioned God's Word and indirectly questioned Adam, the one who had shared God's Word with her. Her questioning led to disobedience. And their disobedience caused them to be expelled from the Garden. "After he drove the man out, he placed on the east side of the Garden of Eden cherubim and a flaming sword flashing back and forth to guard the way to the tree of life" (Genesis 3:24). Adam and Eve were kicked out of the Garden not only because they disobeyed but also to keep them from eating of the tree again. Had they eaten from the tree again, humankind could not be redeemed. By expelling them God was actually being loving and merciful.

Dreams Are Like Prophecies

> After the prophet Hananiah had broken the yoke off the neck of the prophet Jeremiah, the word of the Lord came to Jeremiah: Go and tell Hananiah, 'This is what the Lord says: You have broken a wooden yoke, but in its place you will get a yoke of iron. This is what the Lord Almighty, the God of Israel, says: I will put an iron yoke on the necks of all these nations to make them serve Nebuchadnezzar king of Babylon, and they will serve him. I will even give him control over the wild animals.'" Then the prophet Jeremiah said to Hananiah the prophet, "Listen, Hananiah! The Lord has not sent you, yet you have persuaded this nation to trust in lies. Therefore this is what the Lord says: 'I am about to remove you from the face of the earth. This very year you are going to die, because you have preached rebellion against the Lord.'" In the seventh month of that same year, Hananiah the prophet died. (Jeremiah 28:12–17)

Jeremiah had relayed a message from the Lord to Hananiah that the Jews would be in bondage for seventy years; however, the prophet Hananiah lied to the people saying they would not be enslaved for more than two years (Jeremiah 28:1–12). In Deuteronomy 13:1–5, God explains what needs to be done to false prophets who encourage rebellion with their lies—they must be put to death. Hananiah died as punishment for his lie. This is quite disturbing since Hananiah's name means "grace." But Satan used him as someone familiar to the people to get them to believe a contradicting word.

While God can sometimes reveal things to us through dreams, we should not ask him to do so; rather, we should let God do the revealing in his own way and time. Satan can also visit through dreams, and when he does, dreams can become perverted. For example, when people struggle with lust, it is often because Satan first visited through a dream. He knows that when our dreams are filled with lust, we are headed towards destruction—his intended end.

Prophecies and dreams can only be considered as coming from God if they are supported by the Word of God. We can learn to discern if a dream teaches us do something God would be pleased with, or if the dream has infected our mind with enticements to do something against God's will.

Satan is a roaring lion seeking whom he can destroy (1 Peter 5:8).

- He comes when we are weak, frustrated, and easily persuaded.
- He causes us to rebel against God's authority.
- He wants us to live in total lawlessness.

Lawlessness Is the Attitude of Rebellious People

Lawlessness is rebellion—total disregard for God, his Word, and his established authority. Lawlessness is the attitude of rebellious people. Rebellion against God results when we neither fear God nor desire his authority over us or his will for our lives. Rebellious people refuse to be restrained. They live as if their desires and wills are far superior to God's. They live as if God never spoke.

If we are consistently rebellious, God will remove his authority over us, and we will become our own ruler—something that was never God's intention. Satan knows God has an order of authority. We know this from the way he schemed with Eve. If she lacked trust in and ultimately rejected Adam, whom God had placed in authority over her, there would then be nothing and no one to protect her.

When Satan comes knocking, you can be sure he has an agenda, and that is to use a believer as his pawn, an extension of his evil work. There is nothing more heartbreaking than the Enemy's using someone who was once under Truth. We tend to be so conscious of Satan hijacking the pulpit that we sometimes forget about what he can do through people in the pews. Satan understands that if we question God then we end up being left with our own imagination, a place he always attacks and confuses so that we can't discern things properly. This is why our minds must be sober to win the spiritual battle (1 Peter 1:13–16).

When Jesus explained that he had to go to Jerusalem to suffer and die for humanity, Peter said, "Never, Lord! This shall never happen to you!" Jesus was able to see past Peter's emotions and innocence and recognize that Satan was trying to get him to stumble by speaking through Peter. He turned and said to Peter, "Get behind me, Satan! You are a stumbling block to me; you do not have in mind the concerns of God, but merely human concerns" (Matthew 16:22–24 NIV). We must discern when someone is a stumbling block to us. If we fail to discern, there will be consequences, for Satan demands a price for anything he uses.

Propaganda

Because the Serpent is supernatural, we can't outsmart him, yet we must resist him. There are some things we need to consider when Satan shows up: First, why would Satan lie? Second, does he present his lie to cause us to fall? Third, what does Scripture say about Satan's tactics? These three questions need biblical answers.

The Safest Place in the World

The safest place in all the world is inside the will of God because God is with us, and his grace empowers us; however, we must not believe that we are untouchable when we are inside the will of God. That is never true. In fact, we are much more attractive to Satan when we are living on the inside than on the outside, for Satan wants to see how devoted we are to the will of God.

The game Satan played in the Garden of Eden is the same one he plays today. He sought to take advantage of Adam and Eve because they were in God's will. Adam and Eve were content as long as they understood that their work in the Garden was about God's glory, but they fell when the Serpent convinced them that it was created solely for their pleasure. For Satan's plan to succeed, then, his first ploy involves a word fused with propaganda.

What Is Propaganda?

Propaganda is derogatory information of a biased and misleading nature used to promote a particular point of view. Propaganda is information or ideas spread to influence people's opinion, especially by not giving them all the facts or by secretly emphasizing only selected facts. Satan found out in the Garden that he can entice us to do something by using propaganda. When the Serpent began talking, it was the first time humans were ever tempted, and it is still true today that anytime the Serpent begins talking, we are being tempted.

In the Garden Satan used a ploy; he waited until the woman was alone. Satan speaks to us privately today as well, as he does not want our thoughts to be exposed. Satan preyed upon Eve because she had no direct revelation from God. Adam was the one who had told her what God said. Eve had an indirect revelation, so Satan pursued her rather than go to Adam. The Serpent did not begin by saying, "Do you believe Adam?" Instead, he asked her if she believed God, which undermined Adam's authority. Satan knew that if Eve didn't believe God then Adam's instructions to her were irrelevant.

There are two types of tests/temptations in Scripture:

- One we know comes from God, known as *peirasmos*. This means a trial or test but is often used in Scripture as a temptation. This temptation, however, is positive. James says this type of temptation will produce endurance in us: "Consider it pure joy, my brothers and sisters, whenever you face trials of many kinds, because you know that the testing of your faith produces perseverance" (James 1:2–3).
- A second type of temptation is one we should not entertain. In James 1:13–15 we read, "When tempted, no one should say, 'God is tempting me.' For God cannot be tempted by evil, nor does He tempt anyone. But each

one is tempted when by his own evil desires, he is lured away and enticed. Then after desire has conceived, it gives birth to sin; and when sin is full-grown, gives birth to death."

When God tests us, Satan tempts us. God's test *can* cause us to become weakened. When we respond in the wrong way, we open the door for Satan's temptation. Temptation is an enticement to do evil. We must never forget that when Satan talks, he speaks lies to convince us to do evil and to violate the Word of God. It is an allurement to miss the mark, a solicitation to become independent of the will and the requirement of God.

Think about it: Why are we in God's will? It is not because of his Word? That is why after God gives a Word, Satan shows up to whisper, "Has God indeed said...?" Satan hooked Eve by creating suspicion in her thinking. There was an underlying assumption that maybe God did not say what Eve thought he said. His question left room for her to come up with her own opinion—and that form of the Devil's propaganda is still popular today.

If God's Word Is Not True, There Is No Need for Satan to Lie

But how did Satan know what God said? Satan always shows up on the scene when God is speaking a Word to us. He listens actively and plots a way to get us to totally disregard what God said. He does this with his lies. A lie distorts what is true and always piggybacks off the truth.

If God's Word were not true, there would be no need for Satan to lie. He never denies that God spoke, but he always wants us to question what he spoke about. Eve's response to "Did God really say...?" was: "We may eat fruit from the trees in the garden, but God did say, You must not eat fruit from the tree that is in the middle of the garden, and you must not touch it, or you will die." (Genesis 3:2–3). Eve had been content with the rules and restrictions because she knew they were the will of God, but once Diablos started talking, she no longer accepted the will of God. She thought she was being unfairly restricted. In the same way, Satan can make things seem unfair in our eyes.

When Satan tempts us, he wants us to make the same decision he did. He no longer wanted to be a cherubim because he felt like he was being restricted. He wanted to be like God.

There are five levels of deception, each one being harder than the previous one to be delivered from:

1. When Satan deceives us in our mind.
2. When we are deceived by others.
3. When we are deceived by sin.
4. When we are self-deceived. Demosthenes, a famous Greek orator, said "Nothing is so easy as to deceive one's self; for what we wish, we readily believe."
5. When God deceives us. If we do not think God sends strong delusions, then we are deceived right now. God sends people delusions so they will believe a lie, because they do not want to believe God's truth: "For this reason God sends them a powerful delusion so that they will believe the lie" (2 Thessalonians 2:11).

We never want to get to the fifth level of deception. When Satan is trying to get into our head by speaking in our ear, we will need God's Word to help us overcome. Satan has an objective, and he will only get louder until we fail.

Perversion* of Adam and Eve

Because Satan likes to duplicate God, he created a counterfeit system. Take a look at what he created. God has a rank and a kingdom, and so does Satan. The same applies with the Holy Spirit, who was hovering over the earth, and who now lives in us and is God's gift to us. It is the Holy Spirit who helps us be more conformed to Christ's image. To counter this great gift Satan has his seducing spirit, or lying spirit. This chief spirit is strong and brings manifestations while communicating Satan's lies. The Holy Spirit turns us to Christ while Satan's seducing spirit turns us back to ourselves so the flesh may be glorified.

Satan tempted Eve and then moved her to perversion. In Genesis 3:1, Satan probed Eve by asking, "Did God really say you must not eat the fruit from any of the trees in the garden?" As we know, she responded, "Of course we may eat fruit from the trees in the garden." Where is the mistake in her response? In the third verse, she adds, "It's only the fruit from the tree in the middle of the garden that we are not allowed to eat. God said, 'You must not eat it or even touch it; if you do, you will die.'"

---

* Perversion is the alteration of something from its original course and meaning to a distortion of what was first intended.

Satan never mentioned a specific tree; he only asked if God said they could not eat from "any of the trees in the garden." His question was designed to plant a seed of doubt in Eve in order to undermine the goodness of God. God had told them they could *freely* eat from *all* the trees in the garden but one (Genesis 2:16), but in answering Satan's question Eve replied, "From the fruit of the trees of the garden we may eat" (Genesis 3:2). She omitted the words *freely* and *all*. Satan had caused Eve to forget about all God had said they could have (the positives) and focus only on what he said they could not have (perceived negatives). Subtracting from God's Word will cause one to magnify God's restrictions and minimize his freedom. Not only did Eve subtract from what God said; she added to it too. God never told Adam he couldn't touch the tree; he just told them not to eat of it. Eve's perception moved her from liberty to autonomy, the Devil's breeding ground. Following orders from God does not mean we forfeit liberty! God knows that what is off limits to us potentially will destroy us; still our flesh does not like being governed.

WARNING

Eve opened up the door for deception when she responded to Satan's invitation to dialogue, unwittingly paving the way for a toxic conversation. We must never allow the Enemy to think we are open to suggestion!

The Ways Satan Oppresses

Any time there is adding to and subtracting from the Word, we know there is a spirit other than the Holy Spirit who is at work. God spoke often about the danger of adding to or subtracting from the Word: "Do not add to what I command you and do not subtract from it, but keep the commands of the LORD your God that I give you" (Deuteronomy 4:2); "See that you do all I command you; do not add to it or take away from it" (Deuteronomy 12:32); "Every word of God is flawless; he is a shield to those who take refuge in him. Do not add to his words, or he will rebuke you and prove you a liar" (Proverbs 30:5–6 NIV); "I warn everyone who hears the words of the prophecy of this scroll: If anyone adds anything to them, God will add to that person the plagues described in this scroll. And if anyone takes words away from this scroll of prophecy, God will take away from that person any share in the tree of life and in the Holy City, which are described in this scroll" (Revelation 22:18–19). Satan attempted to mislead Jesus in the wilderness by adding to the Word of God (Matthew 4:5–6). Satan's counterfeit spirit uses alternative schemes to divert, twist, change, or turn something that seems right into something perverted.

The seducing spirit knows that in order to deceive it must move us to believe a lie that would produce perversion. Homosexuality is an example. There is nothing wrong with God's design for man and woman. But a spirit can seduce a person's thoughts so that they accept perversion. People seduced by Satan's lies will agree with something they once knew was wrong. Certainly the Seducer did not stop his lies in the Garden; unruly hearts will always try to justify perversion.

The church at Corinth was very intellectual, and Paul loved them dearly. But believers there never allowed what they heard to change them. For this Paul spoke to them as if they were children (1 Corinthians 3:1–3). And although Paul made it his mission to make sure they remained pure until God brought them home, there was still something he feared—that is, that they would deviate from the true gospel to a counterfeit one.

When Satan tempts, he first does it through oppression. This means he will squeeze and overwhelm us so we cannot make the right decision. People who are oppressed cannot think clearly. To oppression he adds persuasion to move us to decide things when the mind cannot function properly. Since temptation does not work on a heart that is at peace and able to think clearly, it comes when we are angry, discouraged, confused, and discontented.

Why does Satan oppress us? So we may carry out his objectives. How does it begin? All oppression starts when Satan's voice is translated into our own words. In the Garden he knew an animal couldn't get through to Adam because Adam had authority over creation, so he decided to convince Eve instead. When he tries to convince us, we might think we have gained a new friend. But just as he did with Eve, he will leave us once the damage has been done.

Anyone under Satan's deception becomes easy to manipulate. Thought manipulation can lead to thought ruin. How do one's thoughts become ruined? *Noema*. This Greek word refers to a thought in the mind that functions as a final output or perception. In 2 Corinthians 11:3, Paul feared that "somehow your pure and undivided devotion to Christ will be corrupted, just as Eve was deceived by the cunning ways of the serpent." One's thoughts become ruined because devotion to Christ becomes defiled. Only a mind that is undivided and fully devoted to God can produce obedience. This is why Satan wants to distract us. And just as he did with the Corinthians, he will use ingenious messengers against us to spoil our minds. The job of the tempter was to kill everything Paul labored for. In Galatians 4:11, the Apostle wrote, "I fear for you. Perhaps all my hard work with you was for nothing."

Remain in Me, and I Will Remain in You

If we can't neglect our salvation, why would Paul be worried that his work might be in vain? The answer is that it is indeed possible to forsake what we once had if Satan gets hold of us. We see this very thing in the life of Demas. He was once a fellow co-laborer of Paul and Luke (Philemon 1:24). But over time, the love of the world entered his heart, and he abandoned Paul and the gospel: "Demas has deserted me because he loves the things of this life and has gone to

Thessalonica...." (2 Timothy 4:10 NLT). The Greek word for deserted or abandoned is *egkataleipō*. It means to quit, to leave in straits, to entirely abandon, to give up or renounce. Demas did not merely forsake Paul in his hour of need; he renounced him and totally rejected the requirement of walking with Christ—suffering. James mentions in his epistle that those who become friends with the world make themselves an enemy with the Lord (James 4:4). We should not live life as if we could never forfeit our salvation. Moreover, Jesus stressed the importance of true believers abiding in him, or else danger was looming. The book of John records the Lord's words:

> I am the true grapevine, and my Father is the gardener. He cuts off every branch of mine that doesn't produce fruit, and he prunes the branches that do bear fruit so they will produce even more. You have already been pruned and purified by the message I have given you. Remain in me, and I will remain in you. For a branch cannot produce fruit if it is severed from the vine, and you cannot be fruitful unless you remain in me.
>
> Yes, I am the vine; you are the branches. Those who remain in me and I in them will produce much fruit. For apart from me you can do nothing. Anyone who does not remain in me is thrown away like a useless branch and withers. Such branches are gathered into a pile to be burned (John 15:1–6 NLT).

Jesus uses the words "cuts off," or some translations say "to take away" or "lift up." In Greek the word is *airō*. It means to move from its place, to take by force from another what was his and what was committed to him. I have heard many say the verse is speaking of individuals who were not true believers in the first place. But this overlooks that *airō* speaks about individuals who were saved in the beginning but didn't continue to abide in Christ; therefore, they lost what was theirs and what was committed to them. Furthermore, how can someone be cut off from the vine if they were never connected to the vine?

Understanding these verses and others is crucial to keeping our minds clear from popular but misleading interpretations. In this Scripture we also read, "Remain in me, and I will remain in you." The word *remain* or *abide* comes from the Greek word *menō*. It means to continue in a fixed place; to remain in a certain position for a period of time. Why would Jesus warn "false branches" to abide if they were not true branches in the first place?

Some mistakenly think Jesus is promising that a believer's salvation is unconditionally secured. The issue is not the eternal security of believers but whether that security is either conditional or unconditional. Jesus said,

> I have already told you, and you don't believe me. The proof is the work I do in my Father's name. But you don't believe me because you are not my sheep. My sheep listen to my voice; I know them, and they follow me. I give them eternal life, and they will never perish. No one can snatch them away from me, for my Father has given them to me, and he is more powerful than anyone else. No one can snatch them from the Father's hand. The Father and I are one" (John 10:25–30 NLT).

It is important to point out that the words *listen*, *know*, and *follow* in the Greek are present-tense words. They point to action that is habitual and continuous, therefore reflecting a consistent lifestyle. When these present tense words are combined with the indicative mood, as is true of this passage, it represents something that is contemporaneous in action, opposed to action in the past or present. Looking at this verse through the lens of these Greek verbs changes our view. Jesus is saying that eternal security belongs to those who are continually hearing, following, and obeying him. Satan takes pleasure when believers think they are unconditionally secured but are failing to continue to obey Christ's commands. A mindset like this will eventually have one sinning habitually because the person thinks what he or she gained a long time ago can never be taken away.

It is also important that we never become offended by those whom God uses to bring us to our spiritual senses. When we become offended by someone, we lose respect for that person. Perhaps Eve, like us today, was offended by a command she thought was too restrictive or by what she considered unfair. In that case, she lost respect for God and what he commanded of her and Adam.

When the Mind Gets Twisted

The spirit of perversion is sweeping throughout our nation, and it is twisting minds. By the time one's mind is twisted, it is already too late for most people. When Eve ate of the fruit in the Garden and nothing happened, she was deceived. But her disobedience had a greater consequence for Adam because he talked to God directly. If we walk with God, we will face a season of temptation; we cannot stop it. Being tempted itself is not sin but rather how we respond to temptation. And if we cannot pass the season in which our mind is an open target, God will not trust us with much of anything. We cannot fail in our own temptations in the wilderness and still obtain the power Jesus received.

PERCEPTION AND PERSPECTIVE

Now that we have seen the perversion of Adam and Eve, we realize that perversion such as theirs cannot reach its final destination (the ultimate objective of perversion) unless two things change—perspective and perception. In Genesis 3, when Satan saw that Eve could be deceived, he went for her spiritual jugular vein. In verse four, he assured her that she would not die. In the next verse, he informed her that "God knows that your eyes will be opened as soon as you eat it, and you will be like God, knowing both good and evil" (NLT).

Eve Took the Bait

Already believing God was holding something back from her, Eve took the bait. Satan deceived her and caused her to believe that she could become like God. He moved Eve from a *theocentric* (God-centered) view to an *anthropomorphic* (human-centered) view, where the chief goal of man is not to glorify God but to be happy.

As long as Eve was obedient, she was content. God was at the center of her life and mind. She saw the tree, but it was not desirable. But once Satan began to change her perspective and cause her to focus on herself, she desired more. In her selfishness she convinced Adam that what she had taken part in was legitimate, not evil.

Independence, selfish ambition, and self-image are all traits that caused Satan to get kicked out of heaven. These things only build pride, leading us to believe we can be like God. Satan changed Eve's view, and now the tree in the middle of the Garden looked attractive and attainable. Her change in perspective caused her to disobey God, but she did not think of it as sin because her view of sin had become perverted.

Satan Uses Our Perspective

Certain steps are needed to move someone under seduction to their final destination. The first thing Satan uses is perspective. Satan can cause something or someone to convince us that what we believe is okay or that what we once heard was never true. If we know something is wrong and yet pursue it, that is premeditated sin, and a person in premeditated sin can never truly be at peace. How could we surrender to a lie having already been convinced of truth?

Perversion comes from an external force, and it begins with seduction. Satan afflicted Eve's mind by tricking her eyes. When Satan works on us, he causes us to see what he sees, which is always through a humanistic, selfish lens.

When we become humanistic—when our chief goal is to be happy—we become sensitive and disorderly towards anyone who's not in agreement with us. The Serpent knew Eve would be sensitive, so he had to be soothing in order to arouse disobedience.

Satan will use perspective and perception to bring about perversion. Perspective is how we view things; perception is how we understand things. When we are seduced, it messes up our perspective, and if our perspective is off, our perception will be too.

> **WARNING**
>
> Satan's mind games affect how we interpret things. Our perception can become clouded because of preconceived notions and desires (a sense of entitlement, so-called "rights," for example). We can want something so badly that it overrides God's will. If we let it, our perception influences our attitude and we make choices according to emotions. God does not speak to our emotions, but he does speak to our attitude, which is at the center of our will and desires.
>
> In 2 Corinthians 10:3–5, Paul said this about our rebellion: "We are human, but we don't wage war as humans do. We use God's mighty weapons, not worldly weapons, to knock down the strongholds of human reasoning and to destroy false arguments. We destroy every proud obstacle that keeps people from knowing God. We capture their rebellious thoughts and teach them to obey Christ (NLT)."
>
> The "strongholds of human reasoning." Since human reasoning is set, there has to be a confrontation, a conflict, in order to bring about change. Well, a worldly mindset (making decisions from a selfish perspective) is in direct conflict with discernment (making decisions from a godly perspective). If God's perspective is not first in our lives, we will never properly discern.

A Godly Perspective Produces Discernment

In spite of our perverted minds, God knocks down strongholds of human reasoning and destroys false arguments. He does this to correct vain imaginations—things that are not reality. The danger of living out of the imagination is that we are not able to discern.

When Satan plays with our mind, his mind games affect how we interpret things. A seducing spirit can influence a person to notice that things aren't going their way, produce a bad attitude that stems from selfishness, and then persuade the person to act on those negative feelings.

God grows us in difficulties. He strategically designs circumstances where we normally don't do well in order to teach us to discern and to govern our attitudes rightly. If our perspective is not biblical when we are placed in trials, then our perception will not be biblical either.

If Eve's perspective was changed (she was deceived) when she was in the most perfect environment (the Garden of Eden), then ours can most assuredly be hindered. A worldly mindset (making decisions from a selfish perspective) is the exact opposite of discernment (making decisions from God's perspective). We must be of sound mind in order to make careful distinctions as to what is true and what is not true.

In 1 Kings 19:2, we read where Queen Jezebel, angry that God's prophet Elijah had killed all the prophets of Baal, warned: "May the gods strike me and even kill me if by this time tomorrow I have not killed you just as you have killed them." Instead of thinking things through, Elijah grew despondent and fled for his life, abandoning his servant and heading for the wilderness. He even prayed that he might die! Elijah became discouraged and delusional because he saw things from his perspective rather than God's.

Elijah believed an invalid threat based on his own perspective, which led to a wrong conclusion. He succumbed to his emotions and traveled two hundred miles outside the will of God looking for comfort! On Mount Horeb where he had fled, God asked him, "What are you doing here, Elijah?" (1 Kings 19:9). Through an encounter with God on the mountain, Elijah learned that his expectations and point of view were faulty and not at all in line with the way God saw things (vs. 15–18).

Emotions go into overdrive whenever Satan tempts us. The Enemy causes us to become suspicious and to live out our imaginations. We become overwhelmed, discouraged, and insecure, and like Elijah, fail to see things correctly. We might even find ourselves thinking, *I don't remember signing up for all this!* Truth is, though, when we come to God, we do sign up for all this. We sign up to become a target of Satan. We sign up for suffering. We sign up for mountains and valleys, laughter and heartache, crucifixions and resurrections.

The Particulars of Deception*

> The woman said to the serpent, "We may eat fruit from the trees in the garden, but God did say, 'You must not eat fruit from the tree that is in the middle of the garden, and you must not touch it, or you will die.'" "You will not certainly die," the serpent said to the woman. For God knows that when you eat from it your eyes will be opened, and you will be like God, knowing good and evil." When the woman saw that the fruit of the tree was good for food and pleasing to the eye, and also desirable for gaining wisdom, she took some and ate it. She also gave some to her husband, who was with her, and he ate it. (Genesis 3:2–6)

The Serpent made Eve believe God did not mean what he said. His craftiness convinced her to take the fruit and eat it. How could Eve be completely certain about one truth, and then turn around and be convinced about something totally opposite? This was the job of Satan's agent, the Serpent; it is the kind of deception Satan and his

---

* Deception is what we perceive to be acceptable by God according to our own standards. With this definition it is safe to say that people who are under deception also become deceptive.

agents do well. And because of the Enemy's successful plan—including Eve being deceived and Adam being disobedient—everyone was punished by God.

Appearing as a serpent was critical in Satan's plan to deceive Adam and Eve. People tend to base trustworthiness on appearance and speech. Satan was crafty in appearing as an animal believable and trustworthy to Eve. He knows that appearance is the doorway to deception; this is why he shows up as an angel of light, not darkness.

WARNING

In the Old Testament the prophet Samuel almost made a mistake concerning Israel's new king (1 Samuel 16:1–23). He assumed, based on appearance, that the eldest brother was God's choice, but God corrected him, stating that he doesn't judge a man by his outer appearance; he looks at the heart. In the New Testament many missed Christ's first coming because of his appearance. They were looking for a conquering king who would bring them peace and prosperity, not a king who would suffer as foretold in the Psalms and Prophets.

The Function of Seducing Spirits

Deception is extremely dangerous; just because we attend church every Sunday does not mean we are safe from deception. The story of Eve and the Serpent is a clear picture of how Satan visits the church today. In the same way that he appeared in the Garden, Satan shows up and knocks on the doors of the most Spirit-filled churches, intending to get God's people to fall into apostasy. He won't use someone who is considered evil but someone who is sweet, good-natured, and innocent-looking—trustworthy and believable. He is so deceptive he can even get people who have previously accepted Christ to change their beliefs.

One objective of a seducing spirit is to mislead or to cause one's thoughts to wander. When a person's mind starts racing, he is robbed of mental strength and becomes discouraged and overwhelmed (Jeremiah 20:14–18). What Eve saw with her physical eyes gave her thoughts credibility, and she was completely deceived. On the contrary, a sound mind will lead us to believe what God has said despite what we see and feel.

The objective of the Holy Spirit is to convince—to coax us into repenting of our sins and going in the right direction, but we will not change unless we are fully convinced. A seducing spirit, on the other hand, will convince us that we have no need of God. Seducing spirits are rebels against God, and their job is to turn people to themselves and to Satan's agenda. When she was deceived, the first woman became convinced that the things she knew to be true about God were no longer valid.

At first Eve believed what God said, which is why she obeyed, but once the Serpent got through to her, she chose another course. Adam and Eve chose a road opposed to what God had provided. This is what happens whenever people want a perceived truth that meets their expectations—Satan sets them on a course opposite of what God has chosen. The apostle Paul warns his readers that apostasy will disqualify many who have walked with God (1 Timothy 4:1–2).

Jesus himself warned us several times about deception and being deceived. He cried, "O Jerusalem, Jerusalem, the city that kills the prophets and stones God's messengers! How often I have wanted to gather your children together as a hen protects her chicks beneath her wings, but you wouldn't let me" (Matthew 23:37 NLT). The people of Jerusalem had a choice to let Christ do as he said, but they were unwilling. He came to them personally, but still they were not convinced.

Deception, in reality, deals with the lust of the flesh, the lust of the eyes, and the pride of life:

- The lust of the flesh is when a longing or unhealthy craving lies within causing us to be unsatisfied until our desire is fulfilled. It is a preoccupation with gratifying physical desires.
- The lust of the eyes is when we pursue something off limits thinking that once it is obtained, we will be complete. This is the picture of covetousness and why we also see rampant pornography today. Pornography is not an addiction but a spirit. It is called *lust*, which is a lack of self-control. This is not a normal act, and marriage cannot cure it. Burning lust will only intensify.
- The pride of life is a sinful desire for extra prominence or power we perceive we need or deserve.

What is our defense against deception? The only defense we have is to wholeheartedly surrender to the full counsel of God's Word.

Christ the Center

The most important component of our lives is what we believe about God. Our view of God determines what our lives are and will become. Satan gave Eve an alternative to the Creator's belief system. He said, "You will not surely die. For God knows that when you eat of it your eyes will be opened, and you will be like God, knowing good and evil" (Genesis 3:4–5). He convinced her that she could have what God did not want her to have and still be satisfied—that God's belief system was all about Him (God) and of no benefit to her. (Ironically, while the Serpent used that ploy in an evil way, it is actually how life is supposed to be for those who love God (2 Corinthians 5:14–15)). Looking at life through the lens of our needs not being met, it becomes about us and what we need and want. But Christ is the center of all things—the source from which everything springs. He is the reason we live, and we should not mind him saying no to our desires.

In churches today we find that Satan is ever so subtle in his deception. One of his biggest lies is that "God wants you to love yourself." This is Satan's definition of love and is far from the teaching of Scripture. "…Jesus said to His disciples, 'If anyone desires to come after Me, let him deny himself, and take up his cross, and follow Me'" (Matthew 16:24). Do we know what it means to deny ourselves? It is the complete opposite of what Satan is pushing on churches. Second Timothy 3:2 says, "For men will be lovers of themselves, lovers of money, boasters, proud, blasphemers, disobedient to parents, unthankful, unholy." When you are a lover of yourself, you can see nothing else. God never called us to love ourselves! Humanism becomes a potent philosophy of life once the idea to love one's self takes over. It is in fact because of our love of self that we fall short of the glory of God and need a Savior.

Humanism is a system of thought promoted by Satan and his minions. When hardship comes, Satan has us thinking we deserve better than the situation in which we find ourselves. Pride comes in, and we think God is there only to supply our needs and to give us what we want. Friend, God's work will never be complete in you as long as life is always about you and your felt needs. The moment you begin taking ownership of your needs is the moment you replace God.

The Pinball* of Punishment

Relying on God's reputation for being longsuffering, many believe they can be disobedient for a long period of time before they are punished by God. But Adam and Eve were not given unlimited chances. In fact, disobeying God just once cost all of humanity! Considering the hard times we face on a daily basis, we find ourselves wanting to ask Adam and Eve was it worth it.

Sin ruined their innocence. When we are innocent, we are naïve to evil. Carnality is absent, and we are totally devoted to God. But when Satan corrupts our innocence, carnality follows. Satan wants us to no longer be connected to that which is pure and true. In fact, he wants us to see and learn things we should not know, or before we need to know them.

What helps Satan accomplish his plan? He appeals to our unredeemed nature causing us to move towards things prematurely. After Adam and Eve ate of the fruit in the Garden, they felt shame for their nakedness and began putting leaves together for clothing (Genesis 3:7). They moved to self-preservation, and their minds got creative in order to hide what they had done. The plan that prevailed in the Garden of Eden is the same one Satan uses against God's children today.

---

* The definition of *pinball* is to move abruptly from one place to another. There is a pinball reaction between our sins and punishment.

Running Away from God

"Then the man and his wife heard the sound of the Lord God as he was walking in the garden in the cool of the day, and they hid from the Lord God among the trees of the garden" (Genesis 3:8). Prior to his sin, Adam had uninterrupted fellowship with God. But after eating the fruit, he knew what he had done was wrong and that he could possibly face punishment for it. So he hid. Whenever we sin, we end up hiding just like Adam and Eve did when they heard God walking in the Garden. There our mind races, especially at the thought of how God will deal with us, and once the mind games begin, it becomes harder to get back in good standing. Instead of running to *God*, we may run to *people* who are also in sin, just as we are, to help ease our conscience.

> *WARNING*
>
> *The first humans had tremendous freedom, but they lost it because they felt restrained. After they ate from the forbidden tree and lost their freedom, they began using other trees as a safe haven from God. Notice they did not hide near the tree they were advised to avoid but behind trees they had previously deemed undesirable and insufficient. Following Satan's plan leads you back, shamefully and at a high cost, to a place you wish you had never left.*

When God arrived on the scene, he confronted Adam:

God: Where are you?
Adam: I heard you walking in the garden, so I hid. I was afraid because I was naked.
God: Who told you that you were naked? Have you eaten from the tree whose fruit I commanded you not to eat (Genesis 3:9–11)?

God knew where Adam was, but by asking possibly he wanted Adam to realize he and Eve were outside of his will. With God there is no forgiveness and redemption until we realize we are no longer in fellowship with our Creator.

When Adam was without sin, he never hid from God; there was no reason to. In fact, being naked did not even concern him before partaking of the fruit. But Adam's response—"I was afraid because I was naked"— clearly indicates that his innocence was gone. Guilt was alive in his conscience.

FOR GREATER UNDERSTANDING

God gave Adam the command to multiply, but since he already knew they were going to sin, he delayed their ability to conceive. A child being conceived in innocence would nullify why God sent Jesus to take away the sin of the world. Only by being conceived to sinful man could Jesus be the Redeemer of the world.

The dialogue continues in Genesis 3:12–13 (NLT):

Adam: It was the woman you gave me who gave me the fruit, and I ate it.
God to Eve: What have you done?
Eve: The serpent deceived me. That's why I ate it.

And so the blame game begins. Although he confessed, Adam never took full ownership but blamed God for giving him the woman. When God asked Eve what she had done, she offered a partial confession and implied that it wasn't really her fault either.

It must be terrifying to be interrogated by the Father. But if we run and hide, if we refuse to listen when God begins to speak, we will never be able to see in the Garden a picture of the gospel and understand how God saves us. Even though we would not prefer God's cross-examination, we should never want him to leave us alone to our imagination; that would be far worse.

In 2 Samuel 11, we read of King David and his sin with Bathsheba. David committed adultery with Bathsheba and had her husband Uriah killed, but God did not come to address David immediately after his sins. In chapter twelve, we read that about one year later God sent the prophet Nathan to confront David. For one year David had been made to live with the guilt of what he had done. Psalm 32:1–5 and Psalm 51 give us insight into what was going on within him before the prophet arrived:

> Blessed is he whose transgression is forgiven, whose sin is covered. Blessed is the man to whom the Lord does not impute iniquity, and in whose spirit there is no deceit. When I kept silent, my bones grew old through my groaning all the day long. For day and night your hand was heavy upon me; my vitality was turned into the drought of summer. I acknowledged my sin to you, and my iniquity I have not hidden. I said, "I will confess my transgressions to the Lord," and you forgave the iniquity of my sin.

David's choice to conceal his sins produced great physical and emotional distress. However, in God's time, he exposed David's sins to him, mercifully relieving him of the burden and perplexity of guilt.

We Are All One in Christ Jesus

Just as with our own judicial system, with God there is time between the offense and the punishment for investigation. Upon sentencing, God may choose to relieve us from the perplexity he allows, but a price will still be paid for disobeying him. We cannot allow ourselves to think there is only a longsuffering, merciful side to God, for he is also just and deals with people according to their deeds.

Let's go back to the Garden, where God handed down indictments against the Serpent, Eve, and Adam according to the order of the sin as it happened. Here are the formal charges:

> Then the Lord God said to the serpent, "Because you have done this, you are cursed more than all animals, domestic and wild. You will crawl on your belly, groveling in the dust as long as you live.
> And I will cause hostility between you and the woman, and between your offspring and her offspring. He will strike your head, and you will strike his heel."
> Then He said to the woman, "I will sharpen the pain of your pregnancy, and in pain you will give birth. And you will desire to control your husband, but he will rule over you."
> And to the man He said, "Since you listened to your wife and ate from the tree whose fruit I commanded you not to eat, the ground is cursed because of you. All your life you will struggle to scratch a living from it.
> It will grow thorns and thistles for you, though you will eat of its grains.
> By the sweat of your brow will you have food to eat until you return to the ground from which you were made. For you were made from dust, and to dust you will return."
> (Genesis 3:14–19 NLT)

God's judgment on the serpent accounts for why snakes are so despised. Additionally, the fact that God said the serpent would crawl on its belly indicates that snakes did not always slither. What we see of snakes now is what God spoke in the Garden.

In the next verse we see something very spiritual that we could call the gospel before the gospel. Biologically, a woman does not have seed, so here God was foretelling of a virgin birth. In essence, the Seed from the woman will ultimately be victorious over the plans of the Evil One. In verse sixteen we read of the cost of disobedience inherited by all women who would follow Eve. As much as we are thankful for drugs that ease the intensity of birth pains, we can't forget what caused them or the conflict between a husband and wife in women wanting to be dominant in the marital relationship. This is not the will of God.

Finally, when God charged Adam in verses seventeen through nineteen, the man received the longest and harshest judgment of all. Because of his deliberate disobedience, he had to work twice as hard to see the fruits of his labor. As Eve would experience pain during childbirth, so Adam too would experience pain in his toiling. The sin committed by Adam and Eve ruined relationships and brought judgment even upon creation. First, the ground was cursed; second, it would produce thorns; third, man would toil and sweat; and fourth, mankind would die.

It was because of this last judgment—death—that Christ came to earth—so men and women could be redeemed and judged as innocent again. "God was in Christ, reconciling man back to himself (2 Corinthians 5:19). "So in Christ Jesus you are all children of God through faith, for all of you who were baptized into Christ have clothed yourselves with Christ. There is neither Jew nor Gentile, neither slave nor free, nor is there male and female, for you are all one in Christ Jesus. If you belong to Christ, then you are Abraham's seed, and heirs according to the promise" (Galatians 2:26–29). Because of his innocent Son, the Father no longer considers us enemies.

God removed Adam and Eve from the Garden and moved them to a place that was foreign and strange. They lived knowing they could never go back to what they once knew. But they also lived knowing they had received mercy. To spare the couple from further shame God replaced their clothing of self-righteousness (the fig leaves they'd woven together in attempt to hide their nakedness) with clothing he deemed more appropriate—the skin of an animal (Genesis 3:21). Once again we see the picture of the gospel played out before us—the doctrine of substitution. An animal died in order to cover their sin; in the same way, Christ, the Lamb of God, died to cover ours. God provides for a sinner's redemption, not the sinner himself. There had to be a sacrifice for sin and the shedding of blood to forgive the sin (Hebrews 9:22). If we are not judged, we cannot receive mercy. We cannot know Christ until we recognize that we are sinners.

The Posterior* of Adam

Disobedience is dangerous. It is *choosing* to not adhere to what God commands of us. Some are deceived out of their innocence, and some are weakened because of their lack of understanding, but disobedience is never completely from a lack of understanding. Deception is dangerous too. It is the act of Lucifer, who uses it to get us to disobey God. Deception is a vehicle to cause sin, death, and separation. We should steer clear of deception and disobedience, as they are rejection of God's love and care.

God's Mercy Will Not Last Forever

God's mercy will not be offered forever to people who publicly proclaim God's Word but privately disdain it. God says: "Not everyone who says to me, 'Lord, Lord,' will enter the kingdom of heaven, but only the one who does the will of my Father who is in heaven. Many will say to me on that day, 'Lord, Lord, did we not prophesy in your name and in your name drive out demons and in your

---

* Adam's disobedience moved him from being a leader to now being subservient to the very people he was supposed be leading.

name perform many miracles?' Then I will tell them plainly, 'I never knew you. Away from me, you evildoers!'" (Matthew 7:21–23 NIV).

God's people must guard their hearts from the seed of disobedience because the harvest is spiritual starvation and personal devastation. Genesis 3:17 (NLT) says, "...since you listened to your wife and ate from the tree whose fruit I commanded you not to eat...". God judged the man not just because he ate but because he listened to a voice encouraging him to reject what he knew had come directly from God. Because Adam, the seed of man, did not heed God's Word, everyone born after him would be born with a tendency to want to rule himself and reject God.

Satan broke the chain of God's command (God→Adam→Eve→creatures). He reversed that divinely ordained order. Eve's voice became one with the Serpent, making it a vehicle to corrupt the man. Adam took counsel from Eve when she persuaded him to eat of the forbidden fruit. Adam put Eve in God's position and valued her opinion over God's command. A rebellious person does not care about order or structure; insubordination is what he lives for. Man, the only one who had a direct command from God, lost his authority because he obeyed a contrary voice. But God judged Adam, and there was a price to be paid for willfully rejecting him.

Spiritual Senses on Airplane Mode

Refusing to subject to God's given order is rebellion. A rebellious person's behavior is unruly, disorderly. Their attitude indicates unresponsiveness and an inability to receive correction. That person is spiritually unconscious, or dead. Instead of being connected to God, a rebellious person's spiritual senses are in "airplane mode," where warnings are going out but not coming through.

Clearly, there is something going on in Adam for him to violate a direct command from God. What happened to him? Throughout Scripture God's chosen people were recipients of his correction and wrath because of their rebellious ways. God is loving and longsuffering—of that there is no doubt—but how long should the Holy One wait for rebellious hearts to finally be transformed? How long would *we* wait for someone to finally "get the message" after we have waited a very long time? If we reach that place of having had enough, why would we think that God wouldn't?

Ironically, we can only resist rebellion to the degree that we submit to authority. James reminds us to "Submit yourselves, then, to God. Resist the devil, and he will flee from you" (James 4:7 NIV). Disobedience is an act of idolatry. It shows how much we prefer not to follow God's instructions and rather to make ourselves into our own god.

Stubbornness and Worshipping Idols

Scripture reveals that God was sorry he ever made Saul king "… because he has turned away from me and has not carried out my instructions" (1 Samuel 15:11). Through his actions Saul showed God that his heart was far from loyal. When we do not obey God's commands, our disloyalty lands us in precarious places. When someone is willfully disobedient, he lies. Saul was a liar. God had ordered him to get rid of the entire Amalekite nation, including men, women, children, babies, cattle, sheep, goats, camels, and donkeys (1 Samuel 15:3). The New Living Translation of 1 Samuel 15 continues:

> … .and then Saul slaughtered the Amalekites from Havilah all the way to Shur, east of Egypt. He captured Agag, the Amalekite king, but completely destroyed everyone else. Saul and his men spared Agag's life and kept the best of the sheep and goats, the cattle, the fat calves, and the lambs— everything, in fact, that appealed to them. They destroyed only what was worthless or of poor quality (15:7–9).

At that moment God was done with Saul. He had given him specific instructions, but because of his self-conceit, Saul decided to keep what appealed to him.

> When Samuel finally found him, Saul greeted him cheerfully. "May the Lord bless you," he said. "I have carried out the Lord's command!"
> "Then what is all the bleating of sheep and goats and the lowing of cattle I hear?" Samuel demanded.
> "It's true that the army spared the best of the sheep, goats, and cattle," Saul admitted. "But they are going to sacrifice them to the Lord your God. We have destroyed everything else."
> Then Samuel said to Saul, "Stop! Listen to what the Lord told me last night!"
> "What did he tell you?" Saul asked.
> And Samuel told him, "Although you may think little of yourself, are you not the leader of the tribes of Israel? The Lord has anointed you king of Israel. And the Lord sent you on a mission and told you, 'Go and completely destroy the sinners, the Amalekites, until they are all dead.' Why haven't you obeyed the Lord? Why did you rush for the plunder and do what was evil in the Lord's sight?"
> "But I did obey the Lord," Saul insisted. "I carried out the mission he gave me. I brought back King Agag, but I destroyed everyone else. Then my troops brought in the best of the sheep, goats, cattle, and plunder to sacrifice to the Lord your God in Gilgal."
> But Samuel replied, "What is more pleasing to the Lord: your burnt offerings and sacrifices or your obedience to his voice? Listen! Obedience is better than sacrifice, and submission is better than offering the fat of rams. Rebellion is as sinful as witchcraft and stubbornness as bad as worshiping idols. So because you have rejected the command of the Lord, he has rejected you as king" (1 Samuel 15:13–21 NLT).

Saul spoke a half-truth. He was told to "Go and completely destroy the sinners, the Amalekites, until they are all dead," but he did not get rid of everyone. Samuel knew the truth of what Saul had done; he knew Saul had disobeyed the Lord. Instead of obeying God, Saul and his men had rushed for the plunder, doing what was evil in the Lord's sight. Saul even claimed he had been afraid of the people, forgetting that it was God who had appointed him king, not those under him. Saul knew he had sinned, and he thought that because he admitted it, he could easily go back and worship God. But God was finally done with him and was willing to replace him with someone who would obey.

In today's world we tend to hear the word *witchcraft* and think of séances, divination, enchanted rituals, and other spirit-threatening practices that make up the occult. But ...

> Rebellion is as sinful as witchcraft, and stubbornness as bad as worshiping idols. So because you have rejected the command of the Lord, he has rejected you as king (15:22).

Samuel tells us that stubbornness is as bad as worshipping idols! We are to guard our hearts from disobedience and understand that chastisement comes so that we may walk on the right path. Either that, or we end up like King Saul, who had his royalty and rights as leader over Israel stripped from him. Like Adam and Eve, Saul was on the right track, but when disobedience crept into his heart to do the opposite of what God wanted, it disqualified him and left him with a hefty price to pay.

The Provenance of Disobedience

God is more interested in our character than our comfort, and he does not mind temporarily inconveniencing us—or telling us no—if he knows it will produce eternal fruit. The reason is, we cannot see our weaknesses until circumstances reveal them to us.

- *Impatience* may be revealed when we feel as if something or someone is hindering us from achieving our own personal goal.
- *Pride* may be revealed when we are forced to do something we feel is beneath us.
- *Stubbornness* may be revealed when we are commanded to do something we don't want to do.
- *Immaturity* may be revealed when we realize we can't have our way.
- *Self-will* may be revealed when we are required to do something that doesn't align with our personal ambition.
- *Self-centeredness* may be revealed when we have to serve others we don't like.
- *Idolatry* may be revealed when we must give up something that has meaning to us.

There must be a sacrifice, a giving up of something of value for something of greater value. This is what Jesus did, and we should follow in his footsteps.

> ### WARNING
>
> *Disobedience is more dangerous than deception. The natural order of creation was God → Adam → Eve → creatures. Adam's disobedience moved him out of proper order. Because he listened to the counsel of Eve, all humanity paid the price. Adam placed a higher priority on the voice of Satan coming through his wife than on God's voice, and because of his sin, disobedience, selfishness, and rebellion is inherited by all humans.*

The Root of All Disobedience Is Rebellion

Every weakness on the list above is part of man's fallen nature. And the provenance, or root, of all disobedience is rebellion. Satan knows how God feels about rebellion. He hates it. Because of this we must make sure rebellion doesn't rule in our hearts. In 1 Samuel 15:22–23, Samuel asked Saul, "Does the Lord delight in burnt offerings and sacrifices as much as in obeying the Lord? To obey is better than sacrifice, and to heed is better than the fat of rams. For rebellion is like the sin of divination, and arrogance like the evil of idolatry. Because you have rejected the word of the Lord, he has rejected you as king." Burnt offerings and sacrifices here refer to ancient practices of animal sacrifices on an altar. In other words, God says he wants obedience, not works or offerings.

WARNING

Idolatry is a system of thought in which religion becomes a poor substitute for the truth, reality, and requirements of God. An example of idolatry is humanism. Its system of beliefs center on us and our own pleasure, substituting God's requirement to be the center of our lives.

In following his own desires, Saul was dictating to God what was acceptable—not yielding to what God says is acceptable. Worshipping self instead of God is idolatry, and idolatry is spiritual adultery. God has every right to break his covenant with us because of our persistent unfaithfulness.

***

Consider King Solomon. God warned him not to marry foreign women [who worship foreign gods], but the very women God warned him about became his burning passion (1 Kings 11:1–11). What God warned Solomon not to do he did anyway, and God judged him severely.

***

Jeremiah 42 records the first time the nation of Judah sought the prophet Jeremiah for advice. Before, they had thought Jeremiah was crazy, but now that the Word of God was coming to pass and they were under judgment, the people wanted direction. They approached Jeremiah, begging him to intercede: "Please, let our petition be acceptable to you, and pray for us to the Lord your God, for all this remnant (since we are left but a few of many, as you can see), that the Lord your God may show us the way in which we should walk and the thing we should do" (42:2–3).

Jeremiah agreed to help: "Let the Lord be a true and faithful witness between us, if we do not do according to everything which the Lord your God sends us by you. Whether it is pleasing or displeasing, we will obey the voice of the Lord our God to whom we send you, that it may be well with us when we obey the voice of the Lord our God" (42:4–6).

> God explained to the prophet Jeremiah that if the people remained in the land and did not go and live in Egypt, he would show mercy, build them up, and not pull them down. But if they left for Egypt—because they deemed it safe—they would run into the very sword they were running from. Jeremiah relayed the "inappropriate" message, and the people quickly forgot they had said they would obey whatever God spoke. They told Jeremiah he spoke falsely, set out for Egypt, and even took him with them. They eventually ran into the very thing God tried to warn them would happen. God never lies.
>
> From the beginning the people pretended they wanted a true answer from God when all along they were going to do what they wanted regardless of what God said.
>
> ***
>
> The day Adam chose to disobey God was the day he made Eve an idol. We can never be so focused on what God did not say that we forget what he did say.
>
> ***
>
> You might think you would never disobey God the way these people did, yet most believers are not that far from several people in the Bible who disobeyed God. "...Let him that thinketh he standeth take heed lest he fall" (1 Corinthians 10:12).

Rebellion, open hostility or opposition towards authority (basically telling God no), was the root of both Saul's and Adam's disobedience. Please understand that disobedience is never a minor thing. We will never be given a huge task by God if our track record is one of habitual disobedience.

If we exhibit a history of disobedience, we will not be placed in a position of responsibility in the Last Days. God wants people with faith and people who are faithful. And we do not become faithful to the end until God tests us to produce steadfastness in the face of bad situations. Not only does God test our faithfulness; he also tests whether our faith is longsuffering. If we have a short fuse, what does that say about our faith? What God wants is the faithfulness of individuals who are not distracted and self-focused.

How Does Divination Tie to Rebellion?

"For rebellion is like the sin of divination, and arrogance like the evil of idolatry" (1 Samuel 15:23). Rebellion is as sinful as witchcraft—but how? Witchcraft is rooted in *divination*. Divination seeks to control or manipulate events or people according to one's desires. It is how the Evil One got the angels to follow him.

But how does divination tie to rebellion? Rebellion is when our will becomes more dominant than God's voice. Because there is a disagreement between the Creator's voice and our will, there is hostility towards God. In a real sense, rebellion is Satan worship. (See Matthew 12:30, "He that is not with me is against me.") And it becomes especially dangerous whenever a rebellious individual becomes zealous in holding onto his rebellion.

Stubbornness Is Insubordination

If we examine the discussion between Satan and Jesus in the gospel of Matthew, we know Satan attempted to play upon Jesus' human desires by offering him everything he might possibly want. Matthew 4:8–9 says, "Next the devil took him to the peak of a very high mountain and showed him all the kingdoms of the world and their glory. 'I will give it all to you,' he said, 'if you will kneel down and worship me.'" Satan was going to make Jesus' name great on his terms. Christ knew why he had come to the earth and the suffering it would entail, but Satan wanted to make his life comfortable and free from turmoil. He offered to Jesus "his best life now." He would give Jesus all the wealth in the world if only the Lord would take his route instead of God's.

If Satan were to command us to fall on our knees and worship him, we would not do it. Yet he wanted Jesus to do just that—to disobey his Father's instructions—because to do so would mean he was worshipping Satan. He would make Jesus' name great, his life would be easy, and he certainly would not have to die on a cross.

Even though Satan knows that one day God will free us, he also knows there is something in our character that will allow him to remain attached to our lives. He loves to pull out his playbook and attack in areas where we are known to struggle. It is in these times of struggle that we must guard against rebellion and disobedience. When we are rebellious, Satan can make it appear as if life is better with him.

We also need to beware of our passions and not allow them to override the will and commands of God. To be stubborn is to be insubordinate. When we are insubordinate, we will hear what God is saying and yet respond with disobedience. It is not that we *cannot* do what God says but rather that we *will not*. The word *Lord* in the original Greek is defined as a ruler with absolute authority who therefore demands absolute submission. Jesus is the Lord God, and we his subjects, obligated to obey him in all things.

Is God Hard to Please?

It is not hard to understand why God was repeatedly displeased with the children of Israel. He rescued them from Egypt, a picture of salvation. He brought them through the Red Sea, a picture of baptism. He brought refreshing water from a rock to remind them that Christ is their source. Yet the Bible says God was *still* not pleased with them (1 Corinthians 10:1–5). Then is God hard to please? The answer is no, not at all, but God does have demanding standards, and his standards include obedience and submission.

Many of the children of Israel were idolaters (1 Corinthians 10:7). They acknowledged that God was sovereign but refused to surrender to his lordship. How devastating that people who claim to know God as Savior can wind up in hell with people who never even believed God exists! It is important to move beyond a simple but incomplete acknowledgment that Jesus is the Savior who rescues us from sin but nothing more. Jesus must be Lord, and we his subjects.

Disobedience on purpose is serious with God. Willful disobedience changes our position with God. It caused Adam to go from being a leader to being stationed in the rear. God knows what is best for us. He will never harm us. His way is the best way. And it is foolish to think otherwise.

PREVENTATIVE MEASURES

Satan is persuasive and has the ability to turn a damnable lie into a perceived truth. That is the art of deception—to take what is supposed to damage our souls and make it believable. This is very dangerous because every time we believe a lie, we make it harder on ourselves to believe the truth.

No one is exempt from temptation, but there are preventive measures we can take that will reduce our chances of becoming casualties of Satan. One preventative measure is to know the truth of God's Word. Yet knowledge alone is not fool-proof. Adam had truth, but it didn't prevent him from disobeying God.

What could have enabled Adam and Eve to overcome Satan's temptation? It would have been the application of truth they already knew. Applying God's Word in the midst of pressure and persuasion enables us to be victorious. Every temptation we face is a measure of how much we love God and our willingness to apply truth we already know. The tragedy is that many fall victim to Satan's temptation even though they already have everything they need to withstand it.

God's Holiness Does Not Tolerate Rebellion

Satan knows from personal experience that God's holiness will not tolerate rebellion. It is not something to take lightly. Throughout the

Bible, rebellion was always followed by God's judgment, and his judgment was always severe.

Rather than rebel we ought to view temptation as an opportunity to grow. If we respond to temptation correctly, our faith will be matured. We will see God's written word manifested in our lives. But if we respond incorrectly to temptation—that is, with rebellion—four things will happen:

- We will develop a lack of reverence for God.
- Our relationship with God will be damaged, shattered by our sin.
- As we make selfish decisions and rebel against God, we will take others down with us. We become Satan's conduit to slander and offense.
- We become apostate. This does not necessarily mean we leave our church. In fact, we can be faithful church attenders but still have hearts of defection or revolt—a fatal position.

Hebrews 6:4–6 speaks of this fatal position of the heart: "For it is impossible to bring back to repentance those who were once enlightened—those who have experienced the good things of heaven and shared in the Holy Spirit, who have tasted the goodness of the word of God and the power of the age to come—and who then turn away from God. It is impossible to bring such people back to repentance; by rejecting the Son of God, they themselves are nailing him to the cross once again and holding him up to public shame" (NLT).

Satan Becomes One with Our Thoughts

If we deliberately reject God, the explanation is that we knew clearly what God said and still chose to do what we wanted. If the Evil One has our heart at this last, fatal stage, then we have shut God's voice out. And when God no longer speaks, the evil spirit takes away our ability to discern what is right and proper. He becomes one with our thoughts.

There are five steps we can take in order to recognize when Satan is present, who he is speaking through, and what his objective is:

- First, understand that Satan strikes when we are mentally weary and fatigued, unable to discern. He does not want our minds to be strong and sober.
- Second, be aware that the enemy speaks through people who will influence you to see things from a human perspective, not God's. When Peter told Jesus that he would not die, Jesus turned to Peter and opposed him: "Get away from me, Satan! You are a dangerous trap to me. You are seeing things merely from a human point of view, not from God's" (Matthew 16:23). The Lord was able to see that it was not Peter but Satan who was speaking.
- Third, when God speaks a specific word to us, know that Satan also has a strategy and will encourage us to disobey what God has decreed. This is sometimes seen in well-meaning friends who want to give us [ungodly] advice.
- Fourth, we must examine ourselves to see if we are in the faith. Identify things in our heart that Satan can draw strength from.
- Fifth, learn how God wants us to respond. In some instances, God wants us to be silent, and at other times he wants us to be vocal. When Pilate tried to get Jesus to plead his case, Jesus maintained silence, but when Peter confronted him about dying, Jesus spoke up and called Satan out. Learn to discern.

The Enemy Will Lose

Another measure we can take to prevent becoming casualties of Satan is found in James 4:7: "Submit yourselves, then, to God. Resist the devil and he will flee from you." James also lays the foundation for why we should submit: "God opposes the proud but shows favor to the humble" (James 4:5–6).

What makes submission so difficult is that it is a product of the will. When we humble ourselves, we are bringing the totality of who we are under the alignment and authority of God. When we are submitted to God, there are some things we just won't entertain. In Ephesians 4:27, Paul warns us to "not give the devil a foothold." We should never create an opening or an opportunity for Satan. Eve carried on her conversation with the Serpent far too long. First Peter 5:9 tells us unequivocally to "stand firm against him [the Devil], and be strong in your faith" (NLT). Once we humble ourselves in this manner, we will not have to run from Satan. On the contrary, we will be able to block him when he comes charging at us.

Since we don't know how long the temptation will last nor when the Enemy will flee, we must hang in there and remember that it is never what we see but what God says. When Satan tempts, remember—God gave us everything we need to defeat him.

Prevail in Warfare

Satan did not tempt Adam and Eve because they were sinning; he tempted them because they were in the active will of God. The more we walk in God's design for us, the more we will be in direct confrontation with Satan. Satan bullies by being crafty. He comes at us with something tailor-made to fit our weakness.

When we are being tempted, it may feel like Satan is winning and that the truth is weak. But that is the problem. We jump into the battle in our flesh and start judging the situation as unfair or unrighteous.

In Psalm 18:16, David wrote, "He reached down from heaven and rescued me; he drew me out of deep waters." David realized that nothing he could do on his own was enough for him to "keep his head above water." God was his support. He continued: "You light a lamp for me. The Lord, my God, lights up my darkness" (Psalm 18:28 NLT). When Satan opposes us, it is because he wants us to see things his way, but it is God and his Word that illuminates us and lights our path.

When Satan Starts to Squeeze

We are to stand still until we see the salvation of God. When the children of Israel were squeezed by Pharaoh's army, God gave them room to breathe. When Satan makes it dark, God lights the way. God makes sure we walk right in the light so we will not walk in the wrong direction. In Psalm 18, we read that God gives us grace to do things we normally would not be able to do on our own. One thing we can do now is see the spiritual warfare that is all around us.

We don't learn spiritual warfare until we're right there in the thick of it, and that's when we learn to fight God's way. The Adversary is not impressed by how loud we pray and praise but is moved by our steadfastness. To refuse to change directions—to stand firm and remain constant in choosing God's way in all things is a powerful and effective way to oppose the Enemy.

When we walk with God, we walk right into Satan himself. This is part of the believer's life. You see, God didn't save us to put us on a Christian playground; he trains us up to go to war on a battlefield riddled with hostile adversaries, and you can be sure that we will engage in hand-to-hand combat with the Enemy (Ephesians 6:12).

So how do we prevail in warfare? "Blessed be the Lord my Rock, who trains my hands for war, and my fingers for battle" (Psalm 144:1). We don't know how to fight, but God trains us and teaches us by guiding us and "coaching us" through seasons of loss and defeat. We may get discouraged. We may get battered and bruised. His training is not for cowards or whiners. Training is hard, but by obeying the principles and foundations God has laid out for us, we will be victorious.

God Wants Us Faithful, Available, and Teachable

When we take what we know intellectually and live it out experientially, there is application, that leads to alteration, that leads to maturation. We are fully mature when we become FAT: faithful, available, and teachable.

- Faithful = consistently and wholeheartedly doing whatever God commands
- Available = letting go of our own will and submitting to the Lord's purposes
- Teachable = remaining humble

We cannot be FAT if we only can receive corrective instruction from certain people. God used a donkey—an animal considered stubborn by nature—to warn Balaam and refrain him from moving forward, but the prophet was unable to recognize the warning of God because he was driven by his own will. His ambition was greater than his submission (Numbers 22:21–39).

One of the first things God teaches us in spiritual warfare is how to take orders. First Peter 5:8 warns: "Be alert and of sober mind. Your enemy the devil prowls around like a roaring lion looking for someone to devour." If we fail to follow the battle plans of our Commander, we will be devoured. But the apostle Paul told his disciple Timothy to "Be strong through the grace that is in Christ Jesus" (2 Timothy 2:1). God's sanctifying grace enables us to supernaturally achieve things that naturally we could not.

A soldier who gets tied up in the affairs of civilian life cannot please the person who enlisted him (2 Timothy 2:4). Boot camp is specifically designed to break the will of former civilians. A soldier gives up the right to control his own life. Suffering and submission are hallmarks of a great soldier. When we call upon Jesus as our Savior, He becomes our commanding officer and we become his faithful, available, teachable soldiers.

FOR GREATER UNDERSTANDING

For two years the apostle Paul was chained to a Roman soldier, but he never lost heart. He understood that God's purpose was bigger than the situation he was in. He knew that it was God who had ordained his imprisonment in order that he might teach us how to overcome our Adversary. As Paul daily observed the Roman soldier, the Holy Spirit revealed truths to him that he faithfully wrote in letters to the believers in Ephesus.

For the Roman soldier it was always about being prepared. Before a young man could become a Roman soldier he had to pledge his life to the emperor—be willing to die for him, if necessary. (Sound familiar?) They had to train even when there was no war. Soldiers were outfitted with equipment to protect them from their head down to their feet. Let's take a look at three particular pieces of armor:

First, Paul says to "Stand your ground, putting on the belt of truth and the body armor of God's righteousness" (Ephesians 6:14 NLT). Technically, a belt was not considered armor, but it was essential because without it, the other parts of the armor would be unsecured. The belt allowed the soldiers to move quickly and effectively. Do you think it's a coincidence that the belt of truth is the first armor mentioned? No! Truth has to be foundation on which we stand and resist the Father of Lies. God's truth must be the first thing we gird ourselves with to overcome Satan.

Next, Paul says for shoes "put on the peace that comes from the Good News so that you will be fully prepared" (v15 NLT). Soldiers wore a type of protective shoe called chaligae. This shoe had nails on the bottom that allowed soldiers to dig into the ground and hold fast so they would not be moved in battle. Similarly, Christian soldiers must be rooted in the Word so that when our Enemy attacks, we won't move off course. Resisting Satan happens when we rely fully on the gospel of Christ (the record of his life, death, burial, and resurrection)—not when we are living our lives as unregenerated men and women.

> *In verse 16, Paul says, "above all, taking the shield of faith with which you will be able to quench all the fiery darts of the wicked one." "Above all" is commonly interpreted as meaning this specific piece of armor is the most important, but this is not true. Rather, it means "in addition to the previous." We must be girded with the belt of truth. We must have on the breastplate of righteousness. We must be wearing protective shoes to stand. And now, in addition to all the others, we have to take up the shield of faith. The Greek word for "taking up" is analam-bano, and it means to literally to take something up in order to carry it. It is also written in the Greek tense active voice which means the subject is the one who performs the action. In other words, God is not going to make us pick up the shield; we have to make the choice to do this. When Satan is shooting his arrows of lies, we have to decide in that moment that we are not going to be victims but victorious.*

Athletes Win Prizes by Following the Rules

Athletes cannot win a prize unless they follow the rules of the game. According to Ephesians 6:10 we are to…

> Put on the full armor of God, so that you can take your stand against the devil's schemes. For our struggle is not against flesh and blood, but against the rulers, against the authorities, against the powers of this dark world and against the spiritual forces of evil in the heavenly realms. Therefore put on the full armor of God, so that when the day of evil comes, you may be able to stand your ground, and after you have done everything, to stand (Ephesians 6:11–13).

This is a command, not a suggestion. We cannot be selective in what we wear into battle; we have to put on *all* of the armor of God if we're to stand firm against all of the strategies of the Devil. Our objective in spiritual warfare is to stand firm when what the Enemy really wants is for us to throw our hands up and walk away.

Recognize that Satan not only wants to capture us but everything God has said about us. If he can get us to disobey God, our unfaithfulness lands him a victory. A soldier does not get victory medals because he has been in a fight; he has to win. So win! Be strong in the Lord and in the power of his might. You are more than a conqueror in Jesus Christ, and you serve a God who is mighty to save!!

> "I have fought the good fight, I have finished the race, and I have remained faithful. And now the prize awaits me—the crown of righteousness, which the Lord, the righteous Judge, will give me on the day of his return. And the prize is not just for me but for all who eagerly look forward to his appearing" (2 Timothy 4:7–8).

About the Author

Tavares Robinson is the founder and senior pastor of Sound the Trumpet Ministries of Miami in Miami, Florida. He currently serves as the founder of Watchman Publishing. Robinson is also the author of *Shepherds, Hirelings, and Dictators: How to Recognize the Difference*, and *The Utopia of a Strange Love: When the Love of God is Mishandled*.

The Lord has graced him to speak with a bold, prophetic voice that turns the hearts of people back to God. Robinson currently lives with his family in South Florida.

Watchman Publishing
www.watchmanpublishing.com
1-800-714-3194
info@tavaresrobinson.org

OTHER TITLES BY TAVARES ROBINSON

Shepherds, Hirelings and Dictators: How to Recognize the Difference
ISBN 978-1936076277

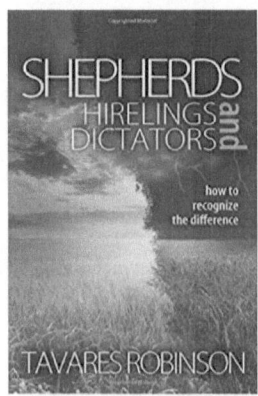

Throughout generations, false prophets and insincere teachers have always pretended to have the best interests of God's people in mind. They claim they are human instruments who have received direct words of the Lord through the Holy Spirit. But in the final analysis, they do not represent God, and they harm the sheep. In this book, Pastor Robinson shows readers how to come out of false teaching into God's marvelous light where there is healing, encouragement, and restoration.

". . . definitely an eye-opener and a tool from God to guard the people of God from deception and error."

The Utopia of a Strange Love: When the Love of God is Mishandled
ISBN 978-1732513402

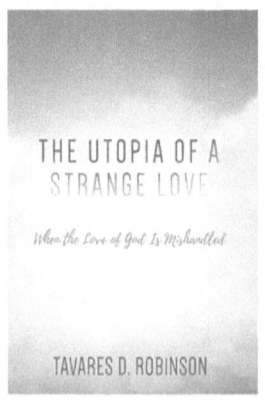

They are ubiquitous these days--eloquent, charismatic preachers, speakers, teachers, and evangelists who skillfully argue that the essential message of Christianity is love. But there are other fundamentals of being a follower of Christ that the popular preachers often ignore. The lack of teaching on it is not just misleading but dangerous. In this book, Pastor Robinson identifies, explores, and discusses the problem.

". . . has changed my walk and view of God. I have more reverence for Him. I want to know what He expects from me!"

www.ingramcontent.com/pod-product-compliance
Lightning Source LLC
Chambersburg PA
CBHW030332080526
44584CB00012B/831